The Acts of the Holy Spirit

THE ACTS
OF
THE HOLY SPIRIT

Arthur T. Pierson

Christian Publications, Inc.

Harrisburg, Pennsylvania

Reprinted 1980
by
Christian Publications, Inc., from the
1895 edition issued by Fleming H. Revell
Company.

The mark of *cp* *vibrant faith*

Christian Publications, Inc.
25 S. 10th Street, P.O. Box 3404
Harrisburg, PA 17105
ISBN: 0-87509-274-8
Printed in the United States of America

Table of Contents

Foreword

At the turn of the century one of the strongest voices for evangelism and world missions was that of the Rev. Arthur T. Pierson. He authored some thirty-five books on missions and the Christian life. Beginning in 1888 he edited *The Missionary Review of the World*, an outstanding and influential missionary periodical.

Arthur Tappan Pierson did his undergraduate studies at Hamilton College, Clinton, N. Y. and his theological studies at Union Theological Seminary. He pastored in Binghamton, N. Y.; Waterford, N. Y.; Detroit, Michigan; Indianapolis, Ind.; and Bethany Church, Philadelphia, Pa.

Pierson enjoyed success from the very beginning of his ministry. He pastored large congregations of influential and wealthy people. His many capabilities distinguished him as a church leader. With all the outward success he experienced a growing restlessness in his own heart. He hungered for such a manifestation of the Holy Spirit as would result in the conversion of sinners.

At the peak of A. T. Pierson's personal spiritual struggle, Major D. W. Whittle and P. P. Bliss came to Detroit to conduct evangelistic meetings. Dr. Pierson attended their services with a burden to learn how God worked in reaching lost souls. The simplicity of Whittle's preaching made a deep impression on this gifted pastor.

Before the close of the six-week campaign, Pierson invited Whittle and Bliss to be his house guests for a month. Before Whittle and Bliss left Detroit, Major Whittle said, "Brother Pierson, Bliss and I are firmly convinced that God would mightily use you if you were wholly consecrated to Him. We have agreed to pray for you daily that you may be fully surrendered."

He could not escape this admonition and began to seek God. The church at his request prepared a private study for Pierson to use as a personal prayer retreat. In that prayer room on November 12, 1875, A. T. Pierson gave up the obstacles to spiritual power in his life and asked God to use him. By the following spring there were indications of revival in his church. On Friday evening, March 24, he shared with those in attendance his surrender to God and asked them to join him in intercession. While they knelt in prayer a fire started somewhere in the building that left their church in ashes by morning.

Using this disaster as an opportunity to implement the kind of evangelism that burdened his heart, Pierson persuaded the church board to rent the "Whitney Opera House" for their services until a new church could be constructed.

The power of God was obvious in Pierson's ministry from the very first service in the opera house. More souls came to Christ in sixteen months than he had witnessed in the previous sixteen years of his ministry. From that time until his death in 1911 A. T. Pierson could be found at the front lines of world evangelism. His studies of evangelism strategy are classics in their field. The Book of Acts was often the resource of his writings. He loved to expound the inspired history of the primitive church. The ministry of the Holy Spirit was central in his understanding of the work of evangelism both at home and overseas. He urged the church to be fully consecrated and filled with the Spirit.

Soon the speaking and writing of A. T. Pierson was having an influence throughout the English speaking world. In evangelistic campaigns and Bible conferences his rich Bible-based preaching was in demand. His clear logic made him popular on the campuses of universities and seminaries on both sides of the Atlantic. Many of his lectures on homiletics, missions, and apologetics are still widely read.

The year 1885 was to bring another powerful

influence into the life of this pastor. He joined a committee to call for a meeting on world evangelism at Northfield, Massachusetts for July 1886. It was at Northfield that A. T. Pierson met Dr. A. J. Gordon. He found in Gordon a kindred spirit and often worked with him in the promotion of world evangelism. The first world student conference in July, 1886 attracted 250 students from 90 colleges. It was only the beginning of a movement destined to make an eternal impact on world missions. From that time Pierson was involved in stirring up missionary enthusiasm among college and university students.

In 1896 Pierson was a principle speaker at the International Student Volunteer Convention held in Liverpool, England. An account of this meeting quotes Pierson as saying that though he was fifty-eight years of age he had recently applied for foreign missionary service. Though he did not become a missionary his contribution to world missions was monumental. By the time of his death 5,000 students had already gone overseas to preach the gospel as a result of the student movement he helped to launch.

From 1891 through 1893 Dr. A. T. Pierson served as interim pastor of the famous Metropolitan Tabernacle founded by Charles Spurgeon. Spurgeon was already ill and passed away just three months after Pierson's arrival. February and March of 1893 Dr. Pierson delivered the annual Duff Missionary Lectureship at Edinburgh, Scotland. That series was published under the title *The New Acts of the Apostles* and became a missionary classic.

After A. T. Pierson returned to the United States accusations were made that he had attempted to gain the pastorate of Metropolitan Tabernacle and prevent the church's extending a call to Thomas Spurgeon. This unfounded rumor brought him great personal grief. At the time this accusation was made Pierson was lecturing at the Nyack Missionary Training Institute and very active as a speaker in Alliance conventions. Dr. A. B. Simpson, president of The Christian and Missionary Alliance, took up Pierson's defense and published a statement in the Alliance magazine which made clear that Pierson was never a candidate in the Metropolitan Tabernacle.

During 1897 A. T. Pierson preached in Alliance conventions in Brooklyn, N. Y.; Boston, Mass.; Pittsburgh, Pa.; and Williamsport, Pa. The weekly *Christian and Missionary Alliance* magazine published fourteen articles by Pierson during that year. During the second series of lectures at Nyack, Dr. Pierson was stricken with illness and the series was suspended. He soon recovered from this illness and resumed his extensive conference ministry. Simpson and Pierson remained fast friends until the latter's death in 1911. Dr. Pierson made a tour of the

Far East that year and had hoped to visit the Alliance mission fields in China, India, and Palestine, but taken ill in Japan he was forced to return home.

The modern missionary movement owes him a debt of gratitude. It has best been stated by Dr. A. B. Simpson on the occasion of Pierson's death:

> "No man of this present generation has had a more brilliant and useful career as a preacher, teacher, writer and missionary leader, and his stamp will ever remain upon the great missionary revival of the present generation in which he had so distinguished a part."

Keith M. Bailey, LL.D.

Introduction

THE ACTS OF THE APOSTLES forms a fifth Gospel, and can be properly understood only in its relation, not alone to the narrative previously written by Luke, but to the whole fourfold Gospel which precedes it.

We have our Lord Jesus Christ thus presented to us in five aspects of His blessed person and work, which remind us of His fivefold "name," as given in prophecy. Matthew exhibits Him as the "Wonderful" Messianic King;[1] Luke as the gracious human "Counselor"; Mark as the "Mighty God," the miracle-worker; John as the "Everlasting Father," in His essential nature; and in the Acts we have Him as the "Prince of Peace," ascended to His throne and sending the Paraclete—the Holy Spirit—as His ascension gift to believers, to conduct in His name and behalf the great work and warfare of this dispensation, the age of outgathering from all nations.

The Book of Acts, however, closely linked with

the Gospel according to Luke, as being from the same human author, is therefore a proper sequel to all the four books which precede it; and may be compared to the mercy-seat which both rested upon and held united the four sides of the sacred ark of the testimony. We may even carry the comparison further; for as it was this mercy-seat, the cover of the ark where the Shechinah fire burned and glowed, it is in the Acts of the Apostles that the Holy Spirit's fire is first seen to burn and shine in latter-day glory.

The Acts of the Apostles should therefore be studied mainly for this double purpose: first, to trace our Lord's unseen but actual *continuance of His divine teaching and working*; and secondly, *to trace the active ministry of the Holy Spirit* as the abiding presence in the church. For it must be observed that Luke's former treatise of "all that Jesus *began* both to do and teach" implies that this latter treatise has to do with what He *continues* to do and teach, in the person of the Paraclete. Hence the discriminating student will here see at once the sequel to the great works of our Lord's earthly ministry, and the record of the "greater works" which were to be wrought by the Holy Spirit after His return to the Father.

The brief study of the Acts which follows is really no more than a first glimpse into a land of promise. It is the announcement of a *discovery* made by the writer that this narrative is a revelation of the Holy Spirit in His *relations to believers as Christ's witnesses*, and *to the church as the witnessing body*; and that from the opening chapter on, there is a *progressive unfolding* of this great theme, which it is our humble endeavor to trace. Nothing is claimed for what follows, save a *suggestion*; like all discoveries, it needs confirmation by a fuller examination and more thorough exploration. But if the hints herein found shall prove grapes of Eshcol, tempting others, who are more competent to search this goodly land more successfully and thoroughly, and lead God's people to its more thorough occupation and enjoyment, the desire and purpose of the author will be fulfilled.

ARTHUR T. PIERSON

October, 1895.

---

1.   Isaiah 9:6.

The Promise of the Holy Spirit

THE REVELATION OF the highest truth needs both words and works for its completeness—theory enforced and illustrated by practical example.

The revelation of the mission and ministry of the Paraclete waited for Christ's incarnation to be fully taught, and for His ascension to be fully explained and understood, when the Spirit was poured out in a glorious baptism of divine energy—a Pentecost of power.

We accordingly find that the great body of our Lord's teaching as to the person and work of the Spirit is found, not in the records of His earlier ministry, but later, in the single discourse immediately preceding His crucifixion,[1] and the last on record, preserved for us in those three precious chapters of the Gospel according to John.

Here the Spirit of God is first known by that mysterious name, PARACLETE, the full meaning of which no one English word can convey or express,

and which, perhaps, it would be better to transfer
direct in its original form into our translation, like
other untranslatable words such as "Jehovah,"
"Abba," "hallelujah," etc. This word "paraclete," like
its nearest Latin equivalent "advocate,"[2] which is
once used to translate it, seems to embody mainly
the conception of being *called to one's aid* or summoned
to act as a substitute; as in a court of law, an advocate
appears to conduct a case or cause in another's
behalf and as his representative.

Whatever other conceptions may properly pertain
to the name Paraclete, this seems to be central and
controlling: the Holy Spirit comes when Christ
goes—comes to take the place of the absent Lord
Jesus; to become, therefore, to the believer and to
the church as the collective body of believers, *all that
Christ would have been had He remained on earth*, with this
added advantage: that as a condition of His
humiliation, the Lord Jesus submitted to certain
limitations of His and our humanity, and was therefore, while in the flesh, not practically omnipresent.
Whereas the Holy Spirit, not having assumed a
human body as His mode of incarnation, is equally
and everywhere resident in and abiding with every
believer. Hence it was "expedient" for His disciples
that Christ should "go away"; for when He departed
He sent the Paraclete to act in His stead.

The fact is both curious and significant that what
is found in the Gospel narratives, in the form of

precept or teaching, reappears in the Acts of the Apostles in the form of practice or example. And so the great truths taught about the Holy Spirit in that "farewell discourse" recorded by John are in the Book of the Acts illustrated and illuminated, being exemplified and applied in actual history.

If, therefore, we are to study the Acts of the Apostles with a view to the understanding of the Holy Spirit's person and ministry as there exhibited, it is first of all desirable and needful to combine, in one continuous form of statement, all that our Lord taught upon this subject in the discourse already referred to, especially as it holds in germ all the teaching afterward illustrated in the Acts and expanded in the Epistles.

We tarry then, at this point, to present the combined body of testimony concerning the Spirit, preserving that obvious parallelism which pervades the whole of this teaching, imparting to it that peculiar poetic rhyme and rhythm of thought which are of the very genius of Hebrew poetry, and help to give insight into the relations of corresponding ideas:

"I will pray the Father,
And he shall give you
    Another Paraclete,
That he may abide with you forever;
    Even the Spirit of truth;

Whom the world cannot receive,
  Because it seeth him not,
    Neither knoweth him:
    But ye know him;
  For he dwelleth with you,
  And shall be in you.

These things have I spoken unto you,
Being yet present with you.
  But the Paraclete,
  Which is the Holy Ghost,
Whom the Father will send in my name,
  He shall teach you all things,
And bring all things to your remembrance,
Whatsoever I have said unto you.

  When the Paraclete is come,
Whom I will send unto you from the Father,
  Even the Spirit of truth,
Which proceedeth from the Father,
  He shall testify of me:
  And ye also shall testify,
Because you have been with me from the
  beginning.

  It is expedient for you that I go away:
  For if I go not away,
The Paraclete will not come unto you;
  But if I depart, I will send him unto you.

And when he is come,
He will reprove the world
  Of sin,
    And of righteousness,
    And of judgment:
  Of sin, because they believe not on me;
    Of righteousness, because I go to my
    Father,
    And ye see me no more;
 Of judgment, because the prince of this world
 is judged.
    I have yet many things to say unto you,
    But ye cannot bear them now.
Howbeit when he, the Spirit of truth, is come,
He will guide you into all truth:
For he shall not speak of himself;
But whatsoever he shall hear,
  That shall he speak:
And he will show you things to come.
  He shall glorify me:
    For he shall receive of mine,
    And shall show it unto you.
All things that the Father hath are mine:
Therefore said I, that he shall take of mine,
  And shall show it unto you."[3]

With this body of teaching before us, we turn to
the Book of the Acts to find the practical example

and illustration of these truths in the early history of the church.

This book we may, perhaps, venture to call the *Acts of the Holy Spirit*, for from first to last it is the record of His advent and activity. Here He is seen coming and working; and all normal activity in believers, individually and collectively, is traced like a stream past its human channel to its divine source and spring. But one true Actor or Agent is here recognized, all other so-called actors or workers being merely His instruments; an agent being one who acts, an instrument being that through which he acts.

This constitutes the unique charm of this book: it is the field chosen for the display of the Spirit's working. To the devout, discerning reader every chapter is but a new channel for His activity, and every event or occurrence a new exhibition of His presence and power in the affairs of the church or mystical body of Christ.

All that remains now is to verify these statements by an examination into the details of this brief history, which, like the story of our Lord's life which precedes, covers the period of about thirty-three years, the average lifetime of a generation, as though to show us for all the generations to come what a power the Spirit would be to the believer and the church if allowed to work unhindered by disobedience, unbelief, worldliness, and carnality.

In this introductory chapter let us put before us the great double truth which we shall find taught and illustrated:

The Spirit of God, the Paraclete, is to be to the disciple and to the church all that Christ would have been had He tarried among us and been the personal companion and counselor of each and all.

And by the Spirit of God working in and through the believer and the church, believers are, in their measure, to be to the world what the Spirit is to them.

These propositions we are now reverently to examine in the light of the recorded "Acts of the Holy Spirit."

The doorways of all God's temples are consonant with the beauty and perfection of what is within; and at the very threshold of this book we meet an indication of the apartments of glorious truth into which we are to enter, and the wonders which are there to be revealed and unveiled.

At the second verse of the opening chapter we read of Christ that He was "taken up, after that he *through the Holy Ghost* had given commandments unto the apostles whom he had chosen."

Here all the blessed intercourse between the risen Lord and His disciples during the forty days between His resurrection and ascension, all the marvelous communications that He made to them as He spake to them of things pertaining to the kingdom of God, are traced to the Holy Spirit. This prepares the reader to appreciate the importance of the commandment immediately following: that His disciples "should not depart from Jerusalem, but wait for the promise of the Father," the baptism of that same Holy Spirit for which Christ Himself had waited thirty years before beginning His public ministry. The disciple is not above his Master, nor the servant above His Lord. If even He was indebted to the Holy Spirit for the power of His ministry, surely we cannot afford to attempt the work appointed us without the same anointing.

This hint of need is immediately followed by a renewed assurance of its supply (we prefer the marginal reading):

"Ye shall receive the *power of the Holy Ghost*, coming upon you: and ye shall be witnesses unto me both in Jerusalem, and in all Judea, and in Samaria, and unto the uttermost parts of the earth."[4]

This is the *initial lesson* which is the key to the entire book which it prefaces. The "promise of the Father" now became also the promise of the Son. The same Holy Spirit who abode in Christ, through whom He discoursed of the kingdom and gave the disciples both instruction and commandment, was to descend upon them, dwell in them, and be to them the source and secret of all power in working and witnessing. So important was this new baptism that for it they were to *wait* before beginning their work—to "tarry, until endued with power from on high." They were to have a new experience, and upon that experience their testimony was to be based, as identifying them with their Master.

Let this first lesson be written in large letters to be read by all, for it unlocks all the history that follows and explains every subsequent lesson. The one supreme qualification of Christ's witnesses is this: that THEY BE ENDUED AND ENDOWED WITH POWER BY THE HOLY SPIRIT.

And the whole narrative which is thus prefaced with such a promise shows us its importance; for here we see disciples, thus endued, becoming to the world what the Spirit has become to them. In them He so incarnates Himself that through them He works upon others, so that by the indwelling Holy Spirit they become, like Him, teachers of truth, guiding into all truth; anointed witnesses, testifying to Christ and glorifying Christ; inspired witnesses, not speaking from themselves, but receiving of the things of Christ and showing them to men; effective witnesses, convincing the world of sin, of righteousness, and of judgment; and even prophetic witnesses, showing things to come.

Thus this Book of the Acts of the Holy Spirit is, with this key, made self-explanatory. The opening chapter sounds the keynote and leading chord of the harmony which follows. What it was that was promised, and what that promise meant, ten days would reveal; and it will best appear to us if, step by step, we follow this fascinating story.

We may anticipate at this point, as properly pertaining to the introductory thoughts, what Peter says in his pentecostal address of Jesus: "Being by the right hand of God exalted, and having received of the Father the promise of the Holy Ghost, He hath shed forth this, which ye now see and hear."[5]

This language, which occurs only here, is too marked to pass unnoticed. The Holy Spirit was God's ascension gift to Christ, that He might be bestowed by Christ as His ascension gift to His church. Hence Christ had said, "And, behold, I send the promise of my Father upon you." This was the promised gift of the Father to the Son, and the Son's promised gift to His believing people. How easy now to reconcile the apparent contradiction of Christ's earlier and later words: "I will pray the Father, and *he shall give you* another Paraclete"; and then afterward, "If I depart, *I will send him* unto you." The Spirit was the Father's answer to the prayer of the Son; and so the gift was transferred by Him to the mystical body of which He is the head.

---

1. John 14, 15, 16.
2. 1 John 2:1.
3. John 14:16, 17, 25, 26; 15:26, 27; 16:7-16.
4. Acts 1:8, margin.
5. Acts 2:33.

The Coming and Working of the Spirit

THE FULFILLMENT OF the mysterious promise of the Father and the Son now makes the pages of this book ablaze with glory.[6] The day of Pentecost found the disciples "with one accord in one place." Suddenly a sound from heaven as of a rushing mighty wind filled all the house, and simultaneously they were all filled with the Spirit; and the first sign of this infilling was this: they "began to speak with other tongues, as the Spirit gave them utterance."

So important is it that every successive stage in these progressive lessons on the Spirit's activity be carefully noted, that it may be well to employ small capitals to make each lesson stand out conspicuously. And so we may mark this first record of His personal working in and through believers—

"THE SPIRIT GAVE THEM UTTERANCE."

That mighty "wind" became to them the divine "breath" which made speech possible. The "cloven tongues" which "sat upon each of them" were symbols of many tongues speaking many languages before unknown; and they were tongues "like as of *fire*," for fire is, throughout the Word of God, the special symbol and signal of the presence and power of God. Mighty as are wind and water, fire surpasses both for resistless, all-overcoming energy.

The Holy Spirit "*sat* upon each of them," to indicate that henceforth He was to find in believers, and in the body of believers—the new church of Christ—His *seat*, His "*see*." We cannot but recall the descent of the Spirit, as a dove, abiding on Christ at His baptism. The dove is a bird that craves a *nest* and a *rest*, unlike the raven, and such others as wander on restless wing. The holy Dove sought in the perfect Man an alighting-place, which He had not found since the creation. And now in the body of Christ, formed out of believing disciples, He takes His abode.

The word "sat" has a marked force in the New Testament. It carries the idea of a *completed preparation*, and a certain *permanence of position and condition*. When Christ had "purged our sins, he *sat down* at the right hand of God,"[7] as though up to this time, like the priests ministering at the altar, for whose sitting down the temple made no provision, His work was unaccomplished, but now He was prepared to rest in His finished atonement and fulfilled mission. The Holy Spirit, also had now found His seat, His abode, to the end of the age in the church of Christ whose true nativity dates from the day of Pentecost. And it is no belittling of His holy offices to say that we are to think thenceforth of the church as a sort of divine cathedral in which this heavenly Archbishop holds His "chair" and presides and from which go forth His subordinate "bishops" or "overseers," to exercise oversight in His name, and the witnesses whom He ordains to do service for Him.

This chapter contains also the first great exhibition and illustration of the *power of the Holy Ghost*.

It is, specifically, *power in connection with witnessing*. We fall into loose ways of using Scripture terms. "Unction" or "anointing" seem to be used quite uniformly by the Apostle John in the sense of spiritual *knowledge*, insight, or the power of spiritual discernment;[8] and here the enduement of power is plainly a spiritual qualification for bearing witness to Christ. And it may be questioned how far we are authorized to refer such terms to other matters, such as the general increase of spiritual gifts and graces, and growth in holiness and attractiveness of character. There are three grand departments of Christian experience—*salvation, sanctification,* and *service*; and unction and pentecostal power appear to be specially connected with the last of the three, giving spiritual discernment of truth, and also, effectiveness in the utterance of the truth.

Peter stands forth as a conspicuous example of this power of the Spirit. He was, indeed, but one of

the company on all of whom rested the same enduement; but his discourse is recorded, and its results
are traced in the conversion of some three thousand
souls.

We are tempted to tarry long over these studies,
but brevity is essential to the purpose now in view;
and we need only note in passing *what sort of a sermon*
the Holy Spirit used as His channel for such converting grace. Nothing could have been further from an
intellectual or literary display. It was no essay or
oration, elaborated with philosophy, decked with
rhetorical ornament. It was a simple, straightfor-
ward address and appeal, in substance a citation
from inspired prophecy, with its verification in the
resurrection of Christ and the ascension gift of the
Holy Spirit.

In view of the wide, if not total, departure of
modern preaching from this pentecostal model, we
need not be amazed at the partial, if not total, dis-
appearance of pentecostal power. What has become
of the *appeal to inspired prophecy* that so little use is made
of it in the pulpit of today? Peter barely calls the
attention of the hearers saying, "Hearken to my
words," before he adds, "This is that which was
spoken by the prophet Joel," and then he points out
the correspondence between the present outpouring and the inspired forecast of it hundreds of
years before. Then a second time he says, "Hear
these words"; and calling attention to the life, death,

and resurrection of Jesus, cites another prediction of David, and again points out the exact correspondence with the facts which could not be denied as having taken place before their eyes. This was really all of this "sermon" as recorded—no introduction, no apparent conclusion; a discourse, if such it may be called, that followed no approved homiletic models and was couched in no enticing words of man's wisdom, neither constructing ornament nor ornamenting construction, but simply putting up two prophecies and placing the events that corresponded with them over against them. Yet such a discourse proved the two-edged sword of the Spirit, wherewith a vast throng "were pricked in their heart."

Is it not time modern preachers resorted to this sword of the Spirit once more, saying like David of the sword of the giant, "There is none like that; give it me"? It is a two-edged sword and cuts both ways. One keen edge is prophecy, with its more than three hundred particulars on record concerning Christ four centuries before His advent; the other keen edge is history with its exact fulfillment of prediction in Him at the time and place predicted. And these two edges converge and unite in a point of power which pricks men in their hearts, and sometimes cuts them to the heart and lays them open to their very vitals.

These are days of doubt and of skepticism that paralyzes men with indifference. Yet he who uses this sword as Peter did, can boldly conclude as he did by saying, "Therefore let all of you know assuredly, that God hath made that same Jesus, whom "men" have crucified, both Lord and Christ." For, if predictions so remote in time and minute in detail are fulfilled in Christ, they must have been inspired of God, and thus they prove the Bible to be a divine book; and if the career of Christ thus exactly corresponds to the portrait drawn many centuries before, He must have been sealed of God, and therefore a divine person. And so the Holy Spirit has given us in one weapon the sufficient answer to both forms of doubt and unbelief now so current—doubt as to the authority of the Scriptures and doubt as to the divinity of Christ.

This same pentecostal narrative likewise exhibits the *mode of the Spirit's activity*. Christ had said, "When he is come, he will convince the world of sin, because they believe not on me." And here is the first example of His operations: He begins His work by *pricking* men in the heart and leading to open *inquiry*—"What shall we do?" Then He leads to genuine *repentance* and the *obedience of faith* so that there is a glad *reception* of the message and a putting on of Christ in *baptism*.

There is a somewhat unique statement in verse 41: "There *were added* about three thousand souls"; and this statement is reinforced by another in verse 47: "And *the Lord added daily* such as were being saved." In both of these passages the best manuscripts contain only the solitary and unqualified verb "added." God cares little for numerical increase in church membership, but much for all real additions to Himself and His mystical body in Christ; and to such body only the Holy Spirit can make any real addition.

Before we dismiss this chapter let us cast one more glance at the work of the Spirit in this new-born church of Christ: *addition, continuance*—fourfold, in teaching and fellowship, breaking of bread and prayers—*community* of interest, *harmony* of testimony, *singleness* of heart, and *gladness* of spirit, while He wrought such wonders and signs through the apostles as produced a strange fear and awe among beholders. Thus, to the *promise* of the Holy Spirit in Chapter 1 are added the *coming, utterance, outpouring,* and *power* of the Spirit in this chapter.

We behold then, in the church and the kingdom of Christ, the *administration of the Spirit begun.* He *forms* the mystical body of Christ and *adds* to it, not in one large accession only, but daily. Later the word *"added"* is changed to *"multiplied."*[9] We have the actual residence and presidency of the Holy Spirit in the church begun, uniting its members in faith, hope, love, and labor, in prayers and all forms of fellowship and testimony. He becomes the source of all true *entrance* upon holy paths and steadfast *continuance* in apostolic teaching and fellowship, and of such mutual sacrifice and sympathy that disciples had "all things common." The rich sold what they had and a redistribution was made to meet the needs of all. Every day became a holy day for its Sabbatic worship and its divine wonder-working.

Other "times of refreshing" are referred to by Peter and the language he uses is peculiar. He is speaking to a Jewish audience and he says, "Repent *ye* therefore, and be *ye* converted, *so that* there may come times of refreshing from the presence of the Lord."[10] The whole passage has been long an enigma to commentators, and the only interpretation that seems to illumine it with true meaning is that which refers it to another and even greater outpouring of the Spirit, which is somehow conditional on the restoration of God's apostate people.

He must be an indifferent and careless reader of prophecy who does not recognize a remarkable future as yet before the Hebrew nation, upon which also hangs larger blessing for the whole race. Thus far, the times of refreshing have come from the *absence* of the Lord, and in connection with the rejection of Christ by the Jews and the extension of gospel privileges to the Gentiles. Other times of refreshing are to "come from the *presence* of the Lord," and in connection with His reception by the Jewish nation and their activity in world-wide evangelism. At least it seems to us the consensus of prophetic testimony. If this be the true meaning of this passage in the Acts, much is made plain that is otherwise obscure: that Pentecost was the *early* rain, and the *latter* rain is to follow even more abundant; the former was on all *believers*, the latter is to be "upon all *flesh*." And hence it was that Peter did not say of that pentecostal enduement, "Now *is fulfilled* that which was spoken by the prophet Joel," but, more guardedly, "*This is that* which was spoken";[11] that is to say, Joel's words furnish the *explanation* of this first Pentecost, though this does not finish their *fulfillment*. In connection with the repentance and conversion of his Jewish hearers, Peter foretells other times of refreshing—the Spirit's latter rain upon all flesh and the times of restitution, or *fulfillment of all which all the prophets have spoken* from the beginning of the age.[12]

This conception of a future further and fuller outpouring of the Holy Spirit, when the long-blinded Jewish mind turns to the Lord, and the Lord Himself returns, seems a necessary factor in the solution of the enigmas of prophecy. Pentecost was the "first-fruits" only of a coming harvest. The Holy Spirit has yet to manifest His power in its fullness and greatness. The latter rain shall be in yet greater abundance.

---

6.   Acts 2.

7. Heb. 1:3.
8. 1 John 2:20, 27.
9. Acts 6:7.
10. Acts 3:19.
11. Acts 2:16.
12. Acts 3:21.

3

The Fullness and Boldness of the Spirit

Satan's activity is always increased when disciples bestir themselves anew. The fires of persecution began to kindle as soon as the fires of the Spirit began to burn. And so, in the next chapter of the Acts, we find the Apostles Peter and John in prison, and then before the court of the Sanhedrin, called to account for a miracle of healing performed on a life-long cripple at the gate Beautiful.[13] When the imperious question was asked, "By what power, or by what name," this deed had been done, "Peter, *filled with the Holy Ghost*," made answer.

This is a second case in which this phrase occurs in this book, but it is now used obviously in connection with *boldness of testimony*,[14] for we read in verse 13: "When they saw the boldness of Peter and John, . . . they marveled." It is plain that special emphasis is designedly laid upon the intrepidity of this witnessing to Christ.

In Peter's case, especially, this boldness was

marked, as his courage was in such contrast with his previous cowardice. He is the same disciple whose denial of the Master thrice and with increasing emphasis, seems in point of culpability and criminality, next only to the base betrayal by Judas, and cannot be dissociated from that damnable act. This man who shrank before a maid and said, "I know him not," now boldly faces the formidable assembly of rulers that connived at the crucifixion of his Master, and calmly says: "Whether it be right in the sight of God to hearken unto you more than unto God, judge ye. For we cannot but speak the things which we have seen and heard." His boldness and courage are thus put in most vivid contrast to the shameful timidity and cowardly denial shown in the high priest's palace. And all this change is traced to the Spirit of grace. More than this, the infilling of the Spirit compels an outflowing in testimony. Before this, Peter could not confess and dared not speak; now he cannot forbear and must give testimony. Like Jeremiah, God's Word being "in his heart as a burning fire shut up in his bones," he is "weary with forbearing, and cannot stay" his witness.

When, from the presence of the rulers, Peter and John return to their own company, and with their fellow-disciples engage in prayer, *boldness* is again made conspicuous by being the subject of entreaty: "And now, Lord, behold their threatenings: and grant unto thy servants, that *with all boldness* they may speak thy Word, by stretching forth thine hand to heal; and that signs and wonders may be done by the name of thy holy child Jesus. And when they had prayed, the place was shaken where they were assembled together; and they were all filled with the Holy Ghost, and they spake the Word of God with boldness."[15]

If it is not designed that the one impression of BOLDNESS IN WITNESS, as consequent upon the fullness of the Spirit, should be prominent here, this chapter in the Acts is out of place. This is the next in this series of progressive lessons on the Spirit's power, and wonderful indeed is the mode of its teaching. Not only is the cowardly and timid denier of Christ turned into a courageous and brave defender, but the whole assembly is moved to pray for "all boldness," and the answer comes at once in the very form and manner desired; and the boldness is traced distinctly to the infilling of the Spirit, as though the fullness within could not be restrained, but like a stream bursting through all barriers, sweeping away all obstacles, must scoop out for itself a channel in speech.

In every age boldness, such as is born of the Spirit of God, is the first requisite of God's witnesses. And it has been the conspicuous characteristic of all those who, like Elijah and John the Baptist, have been the religious reformers of society or special messengers of God's power to His people. We do not appreciate the fact that since the fall of man, truth and piety have never commanded the voice and vote of the majority. Our Lord, in that matchless Sermon on the Mount, teaches us that breadth and multitude always go together, and narrowness and fewness. "Wide is the gate, and broad is the way, that leadeth to destruction, and many there be which go in thereat: *because* strait is the gate, and narrow is the way, which leadeth unto life, and few there be that find it."[16]

This teaching is explicit. There are and always have been two ways: one is wide at the entrance and broad all the way through, and it always has the many; the other presents a narrow entrance and is narrow all the way through, and it always has the few. And it is further remarkable, as an historic fact, that just as soon as any movement, though *beginning* with a spiritual impulse and even in a spirit of protest and reform, gets to be popular and numerically strong, its point of peril is reached, if, indeed, it be not already disastrously passed; and the way that once was costly to enter and hard to follow now becomes easy to enter and correspondingly pleasant to pursue. It is one of the paradoxes of history that the church, born in persecution and baptized in blood, no sooner grows to be numerous and strong than it begins to broaden out its doctrinal beliefs and to compromise with the secular spirit of the age. There is more than one case in history where the same body of believers that once led the way in protest against heresy, afterward led the way in countenancing heresy; so that those who once separated from others for the sake of holy living need to be separated from, by those who would live holy!

Boldness is therefore always requisite to a true witness for God, and it must be the boldness of the Holy Spirit. Otherwise, how can there be a discernment of spirits hostile to God, a discrimination between truth and error, a penetration behind the veil of popularity to the real features of prevailing, teaching, and practice! The boldness of the Spirit is not the rash, impetuous complaint of the cynic, nor the destructive and indiscriminate image-breaking of the iconoclast and universal censor—it does not put a Talus in the church with an iron flail in his hand to demolish whatever exists, because it invites attack. When the Holy Spirit gives boldness it is first of all the boldness that comes of clearness of vision as to the real character of existing customs and opinions; and then it is manifest in a faithful but loving and tender remonstrance, cost what it may though, like John the Baptist, one must give up his head for his fidelity.

No one attribute is more needful today for Christ's witnesses than Holy Spirit boldness due to Holy Spirit fullness. There is in progress, in the world and in the church, a philosophy of *evolution* that not only denies the Scripture teaching of creation and the fall, but would make Jesus Christ simply the best product, so far, of evolutional development; which would reduce the Bible to a mere collection of books, growing in value and virtue as the race made such progress possible, and in turn, to be superseded as new conditions raise man to a level where a higher standard of teaching is both possible and needful! Of course in such a philosophy there is no room for regeneration or resurrection or anything supernatural. And yet such doctrine is rapidly winding its way into our colleges, theological seminaries, churches, and pulpits; and how many are there who have the clearness of vision to see and the boldness of speech to testify!

We have a profound conviction that, were the Holy Spirit today outpoured, or inpoured, in such manner as to fill modern disciples as the apostles were once filled, there would be an instant discovery and disclosure of the destructive tendencies of much so-called "higher criticism"; a revelation of the drift of modern doctrinal teaching toward the breadth of the way of death, and of modern practice toward the manners of the many who worship the god of this world; a new sense of awful peril that would multiply Elijahs on every mountaintop, Johns in every Herod's palace, and Peters in every church court, to utter a mighty remonstrance against current evils glossed over with popularity and respectability.

Take one form of holy boldness—the courageous

indifference to human opinion on the part of him who studies only to show himself approved unto God. How many even of God's ministers, when German mysticism, rationalism, and neology come into Christian churches, pulpits, and courts, in the university gown, *dare* not contend against it for fear of being spoken of as "ignorant and unlearned";[17] and yet that was one of the conditions of apostolic boldness! Men are too anxious to be ranked with scholars; and so when error, however deadly, wears the glittering serpent-skin of scholarship, it insinuates itself into the very chair of the teacher, and the pulpit of the preacher, and no one seems to dare to smite it with a bold blow! And yet it is but needful to glance back over the centuries of history to see that the men who stand out most conspicuously heroic and noble are those who have faced ridicule, hatred, and death itself, for the sake of a candid and courageous remonstrance and protest against prevailing errors in doctrine and practice.

In this connection a remarkable and novel exhibition of the Spirit's presence was witnessed, for "when they had prayed, THE PLACE WAS SHAKEN WHERE THEY WERE ASSEMBLED TOGETHER." The presence of the Holy Spirit was so wonderfully manifested that even dead walls felt the power of the Spirit of life—matter responded to spirit. In all human history there had been nothing like this, save when the house was so filled with glory that the priests could not minister before the Lord,[18] or "the posts of the door moved at the voice of him that cried."[19]

What a suggestion of the Holy Spirit's operations! He did not dwell in those walls, yet they were moved at His presence. Pillars and posts, blocks of stone and blocks of wood may be *moved* when they cannot be *molded*. And here is a possible hint as to the meaning of such words as those in the epistle to the Hebrews.[20] It is not said that those who had thus been "partakers of the Holy Ghost" had ever been regenerated; those who were referred to as falling away beyond renewal unto repentance may never have been born from above. They may have been partakers of the Holy Ghost only as, or somewhat as, those walls, dead, inert matter as they were, were shaken—sharing in the manifestation of the power of the Spirit whom in no sense they either received or recognized. Felix trembled as Paul reasoned and Agrippa was almost persuaded when Paul argued from prophecy; but neither of them appears ever to have become a disciple; they were like the house that was shaken, but unchanged in character. In every congregation of disciples many are also found who pass through scenes of "revival" deeply stirred, profoundly moved, sometimes shaken to the very foundations of their being, but who nevertheless feel the Spirit's power and presence only as the dead walls, pillars, and posts that are shaken for the instant, but not changed in nature; moved, not molded; or as Stephen's stoners, "not able to resist the wisdom and the spirit by which he spake," yet *did* resist to their own ruin.[21]

As this display of the Spirit's power is introduced in connection with the prayer for boldness in witnessing, it was undoubtedly meant to inspire courageous confidence that *God was with them*, few as they were and feeble as they were; and that He who could thus shake the very walls could sway all hard hearts and cruel foes; and, if He pleased, open prison doors, as He subsequently did, and smite with death, as He smote Herod. They asked that they might be emboldened by signs of healing power; the Spirit gave other signs not asked, in shaking walls, that could know no healing power.

One grand motive in praying for divine interposition is that our boldness in testimony may be increased. When God withdraws His hand of power, how our mouths are proportionately closed! We cannot speak boldly if He does not work mightily, for His mighty working is the confirming of our witness. We are therefore authorized to ask in faith for God's accompanying power to attend our preaching, that we may be bold to bear witness, because of Another who beareth witness to us and sealeth our message as His own. Well may it make one courageously and confidently outspoken when God is manifestly behind both the man and his message with confirming power. Nor should we ever rest without such confirming co-witness.

13. Acts 4:1-12.
14. Cf. Acts 2:4.
15. Acts 4:29-31.
16. Matt. 7:13-14.
17. Acts 4:13.
18. 1 Kings 8:11.
19. Isa. 6:4.
20. Heb. 6:4-5.
21. Acts 6:10.

4

The Presence and Presidency of the Spirit

THE WORD "PRESENCE" IMPLIES personality as we more correctly use it. And the fifth chapter of the Acts of the Holy Ghost contains an unmistakable unveiling of the fact that He is a *Person*, present and presiding in the church.

When Ananias and Sapphira conspired in a sin of sacrilege, keeping back in part what, being already given unto God, was to be ranked among "devoted" things, they committed a sin similar to that of Achan, and were visited with like penalties.[22]

The noticeable feature, however, is not this correspondence, so much as the indirect but unquestionable witness to the individuality, personality, presence, and presidency of the Spirit. Peter said to Ananias, "Why hath Satan filled thine heart to LIE TO THE HOLY GHOST?" And afterward to Sapphira, "How is it that ye have agreed together to TEMPT THE SPIRIT OF THE LORD?" Let us mark, also, how he added to his rebuke to Ananias, "Thou has not lied unto men, but UNTO GOD."

Thus, in one transaction so briefly recorded, we are vividly impressed with three facts, all the more impressive because assumed to be facts, and needing no argument or even direct assertion:

1. The Spirit is a *person*, with personal attributes.
2. The Spirit is *God*, not only having divinity, but diety.
3. The Spirit is the *presiding presence* in the church.

If the Holy Spirit were, as some would have us believe, only "a thin and shadowy effluence proceeding from God," as the breath exhales from one's body, such language as is here used would be absurdly inappropriate. It is plain that a man cannot "lie" to an influence or effluence, or "tempt" and defraud anything less than a person. Moreover, it is distinctly affirmed that, in thus lying "unto the Holy Ghost," Ananias had lied "not unto men, but unto *God*." And yet once more, though Peter was nominally and apparently the presiding officer, back of this visible leader was an invisible presence, One who was actually presiding over the church, and of whom Peter was but the organ and representative. And therefore, it was that the lie was not unto men, but unto God, and that in this fraud and sacrilege they were tempting the Spirit of the Lord.

Here, then, we reach another distinct stage in this revelation of the actual working of the Spirit. We are dealing with a *person of the Godhead who is present and pre-*

siding in the church as the body of Christ. And, as has been hinted, this lesson is more emphatic because it is taught without argument, hesitation, or explanation. It is not treated like a truth open to doubt or surprisingly novel and startling, but most natural and necessary. The Holy Spirit is recognized as being the all-controlling Head of affairs, and as though His headship were never doubted or disputed. Any unholy, irreverent, or profane word or act was an insult to this unseen presence. Man was therefore forgotten in His august presidency.

This advanced lesson is one of the utmost importance. We cannot do justice to the Holy Spirit unless we conceive of Him as individual, personal, divine. Those who have no higher thought of Him than as an influence exerted by God, as the light radiates from the sun, have read the Book of the Acts to little purpose. Here He is everywhere treated as a person—personal attributes being ascribed to Him, and personal claims asserted and implied for Him. It is perhaps the main purpose of this book to show, once for all, how it is that He abides in believers and makes the body of disciples His habitation; how He works in and through them, developing holy character and conduct, and guiding in holy service for the kingdom. The more minute our examination of this brief narrative the more plain will it become that all true, holy, useful forms of activity for God, every word spoken in witness for Him, every step taken in furtherance of His work, every plan formed for the glory of God, are to be traced directly to the Holy Spirit as their origin and inspiration.

That the fact of His presence and presidency in the church might be the more actual and awful, it was emphasized by an *act of judgment*. Ananias and Sapphira were both struck instantly dead. Peter had hardly said the awe-inspiring words, "Thou hast not lied unto men, but unto God," when Ananias "fell down, and gave up the ghost"; and Peter had no sooner uttered a similar rebuke to the wife, charging her with being party to tempting the Spirit of the Lord, than she "straightway fell down at his feet" and died also. What wonder if "great fear came upon all the church, and upon as many as heard these things"!

The Holy Spirit is preeminently the Spirit of love and grace, and He seems to have taken the form of a *dove* at Christ's baptism because the dove is the most affectionate of the birds. But He is also the Spirit of truth, and desires and demands "truth in the inward parts." Once for all He found it needful to impress His actual and awful presence, and His jealousy of His own honor, by a judicial infliction of penalty the like of which never occurs again in the record of His acts. This was needful for saints, but especially for sinners. The world sees Him not, neither knows Him; and as He had just "shaken" a house incapable of receiving Him and knowing Him, so now He makes even those who were outside the assemblies of believers and heard these things, acknowledge His presence and power and shake and quake with fear.

But, though no longer such instant judgment follows such sins of sacrilege, is the Holy Ghost any less displeased when nominal disciples lie to Him, tempt Him, defraud Him of His own? God seems to follow a certain *policy of judicial infliction.* Once for all He makes an example of an offender in each of the prominent forms of sin—as of Cain in murder, of Lot's wife in loitering, of Achan in sacrilege, of Korah in presumption, of Uzziah in profanation, of Saul in disobedience—and afterward seldom, if ever, punishes similarly a like offense. His design appears to be to express and exhibit in one startling example His abhorrence of the particular sin which He visits with condign judgment, as if rearing a permanent memorial of His holy hatred of that specific form of evil; and thenceforward forbearing with other like offenders until the day of final judgment, when His long-pent-up wrath will have vent. We must not infer from the rarity of such judgments in this world, or from their solitariness, that God's mind has changed as to the exceeding sinfulness and hate-fulness and ill desert of the sin He has thus rebuked. The solitary example must stand as a lasting and terrible monument of what God thinks of that sin. And to Him who will understand, every such visita-

tion writes on the page of history in letters of flame:
  "Oh, do not this abominable thing
    Which I hate!"

We must not infer too hastily that sins against the Holy Ghost are not now committed with frequency, or that when committed they are always passed by without prompt punishment.

From time to time awe comes upon as many as hear of God's awful inflictions of penalty upon flagrant transgressors. Those who are familiar with the remarkable career of the Wesley brothers will recall more than one instance of supernatural visitations of judgment. For example, during Charles Wesley's revival meetings at St. Just, in Cornwall, England, a country squire, Eustick by name, drove a pack of hounds among the congregation in order to break up the meeting and drive the attendants away—a mode of annoyance not infrequent in those days. On this occasion a number of the Lord's people withdrew and took refuge in a spacious kitchen. The prayer meeting held there was of such extraordinary power as to surpass any other that those who were present had known. And as the service closed, Mr. Wesley, as if endowed with prophetic vision, arose and said, with an awful solemnity and deliberation, "The man who has this day troubled you shall trouble you no more forever."[23] Shortly afterward Eustick passed to his last account in a state of raving madness.

In our own day, in one of our State capitals, a scheme was laid to drive from his charge a godly minister who for many years had served his church with rare fidelity, and whose only fault was that of advancing age. The plot was laid to call a meeting at the close of the Sabbath morning service and compel his resignation. On the very morning when the deed was to be done, and at the very hour, the prime mover, on whom the success of the plot depended, fell dead, and again awe fell on all who heard these things.

In the year 1889 a company of twelve young men, meeting at a hotel table for a carousal, and observing their number to be that of the apostolic company at the first Lord's Supper, actually celebrated a mock eucharist. Before midnight the leader was dead, and every other of the company hung in mortal agony on the verge of the grave!

Another instance may be given of a church in which some thirty men conspired to defeat a pastor's measures for spirituality in church life and administration, and at last compelled his withdrawal to another field. As he left the town it suddenly flashed on him that *every one* of the number who had combined to thwart what he had undertaken in behalf of the Holy Spirit had suffered some form of divine judgment or chastisement. And Dr. A. J. Gordon, late of Boston, a man specially filled with the Spirit, used to give startling examples known to him, where individuals and whole churches which had resisted the Holy Spirit were visited by remarkable judgments. God the Holy Ghost may be silent and apparently indifferent, but *God is not dead*.

In this same chapter Peter says to the council, when once more arraigned for disobedience to their authority, "We ought to obey God rather than men. . . We are his witnesses of these things; and so is also the Holy Ghost, whom God hath given to them that obey him."[24] Here we meet for the first time in this book—

THE WITNESS OF THE SPIRIT.

Among the teachings of Christ as to the ministry of the Spirit we found this matter of co-witness prominent: "He shall bear witness of me: and ye also shall bear witness, because ye have been with me from the beginning."[25] And here this teaching finds exemplification.

There are three points of view from which this co-witnessing may be considered:

1. The Holy Ghost witnesses to us of Christ; that is *revelation*.
2. We witness to Christ by the Holy Ghost; that is *declaration*.
3. The Holy Ghost witnesses to us and our witness; that is *attestation*.

We cannot properly appreciate His co-witness while any one of these is overlooked. We should ourselves truly apprehend Christ only through His gracious help in unveiling our eyes and revealing the power and beauty of the Lord; we should witness to Christ with truth and power only as He endues us for the testimony; and our testimony would lack confirmation and attestation if He did not accompany it with the signs and wonders that only He can work.

As to the place which this new reference to the Spirit holds, in the progressive development of the great theme we are considering, it seems plain that we have here an incidental lesson as to the *philosophy* of the Spirit's working. We have seen Him, from the day of Pentecost onward, working mightily among men, pricking them with the sword of His truth, converting them by thousands, imparting super-natural boldness, and even shaking walls and aveng-ing sacrilege, so that the people trembled with awe; and now we are taught that all this constitutes *a part of His mode of confirming the testimony* of these humble disciples. Few and feeble as they are, the mighty God is with them and giving weight to their witness, by wondrous signs of the fact that they speak by higher authority, and that in disobeying men they are obeying God.

And, further, we have here a positive declaration of the grand *condition* of such co-witness: OBEDIENCE. The Holy Spirit is given to all obedient souls. Consequently *disobedience forfeits* all His most precious gifts. And if His essential power has been withdrawn, if our preaching, teaching, testifying, now lacks in any degree His confirming co-witness, may it not be because there has been a departure from the New Testament models? If for any reason we have "lost our testimony" by conformity to another pattern, or by following our own devices, we have so far lost also His testimony, or attestation, and our witness has become formal and forceless.

There must have been a strange divine sanction attending the words of these poor and persecuted saints. Even the wise politician, Gamaliel, seems to have felt it, and so, from the mere point of worldly policy, he counsels that his fellow members of the Sanhedrin shall let these men alone. For he says, "If this counsel or this work be of men, it will come to naught: but, if it be of God, ye cannot overthrow it; lest haply ye be found even to fight against God."[26] But, while their foes are smitten with awe, the disciples depart from the presence of the council, unawed by the authority or threatening of men, but full of joy in the Holy Ghost, that they might, even at the price of personal suffering and shame, have the privilege and glory of being fellow-witnesses with the Spirit of God to the Jesus whom they continue daily to preach.

Let us not pass on without another reflection over the new lessons we are learning. There is a co-witness of the Spirit, and it is given to all obedient souls. They who, like the apostles, make it their one aim to bear witness to a risen, ascended, glorified Christ, shall find the Holy Spirit adding His testimony to theirs. How? By giving them *utterance*, so that their witness becomes His testimony; and by imparting to them *boldness*, so that even their enemies are struck with awe.

But they had, as we also have, need of some other form of joint testimony to confirm their word, for this could hardly be called a *co*-witness. And we are elsewhere told how the Spirit attested, as divine, their testimony; "God also bearing them witness, both with signs and wonders, and with divers miracles, and gifts of the Holy Ghost, according to his own will."[27]

This was the second appearance of Peter and his brother apostles before the council. On the previous occasion Peter and John had confounded these rulers by their bold witness, and by the Holy Ghost's co-witness in the man healed and standing with them, so that the rulers could say nothing against it but were compelled to confess a notable miracle as having been done. And now, as again they challenge the council to say whether they ought not to obey God rather than men, they openly declare the great truth that *not* to obey would be to forfeit that confirming co-witness! What rich lessons on holy living and mighty preaching here abound!

22.   Josh. 7:21-26.
23.   *Life of Mrs. Booth*, I, 462.
24.   Acts 5:29, 32.
25.   John 15:26-27.
26.   Acts 5:38-39.
27.   Heb. 2:4.

5

The Ministry and Authority of the Spirit

THE HOLY SPIRIT'S ACTIVE administration in the church now has its first exhibition in the form of the *choice of subordinate officers.*

The sixth chapter of the Acts of the Holy Ghost introduces the necessity for the erection of a new office—that of *deacons*, for the serving of the neglected poor; and we are taught that the central qualification is that they be men "full of the Holy Ghost": "Wherefore look ye out from among you seven men of *honest report*, FULL OF THE HOLY GHOST *and of wisdom*, whom we may appoint over this business."[28]

The Spirit of God does not surrender His headship in the church in intrusting to human hands any department of its affairs. Not only so, but all those so intrusted must be capable of cooperation with Him; and therefore they who in His name are to administer affairs must themselves be filled with the Spirit, so that in *their* ministry may be seen the ministry of the Spirit Himself. Even an office that deals with *temporalities* and distributions of money and food must be filled by Holy Ghost men. "Secular men" have absolutely no place in the administration of the affairs of the church of Christ, all of which are "sacred" to the Holy Spirit.

A unique lesson on church life, indeed! Let us lay stress on it, by repetition. Secular men—men of a worldly type of character and a secular spirit—have no place in the church of Christ; above all, no *official* place, though it be only in administering "secular" affairs, and though they be men of both honest report and of wisdom. The natural man, even when that term is used of the princes of this world,[29] cannot receive the things of the Spirit because they are spiritually discerned; and therefore, so far as we put into office or allow to occupy official positions in the church, men who have not the Spirit of God, who are chosen without reference to spiritual qualifications, we at least consent to an administration which is unspiritual in character, which is an offense to the Spirit, a virtual disputing of His headship, and we hesitate not to add, in so far an ACTUAL UNSEATING OF THE SPIRIT from His throne of control!

If this appear to any to be an extreme position, let such consider what, in other spheres of business, is the common course pursued when it is desired to rid a corporate body of its controlling or presiding head. We will suppose a corporation to have a man as president whom for some reason it is deemed desirable to quietly "oust" or displace. Gradually, in the subordinate offices and board of trustees or directors, men are placed who are opposed to the presiding officer in method and spirit. They quietly antagonize his measures, obstruct his plans, thwart his policy. Instead of cooperation and support, he meets inertia and indifference, if not violent opposition; until at last, unable to conduct affairs, he resigns from sheer inability to carry out what he regards as a true policy of administration.

The Spirit of God is like a dove which is eager to alight and rest in the dovecote, but is also timid and easily driven away. He never takes control of any man or body of men without their will. His methods are not compulsory, but persuasive. He may be "grieved" as easily as a tender-hearted parent, "quenched" as easily as a flickering flame. However, forbearing with our childish mistakes and errors of judgment, or even with our relapses into sin, He will not remain in control of an *unwilling subject. Disobedience practically drives Him away.* And when He sees men put into official trusts in the church who are ungodly men, or without spiritual knowledge of Himself and fitness to cooperate with Him, and indisposed or incompetent to administer the church in His name and according to His mind, is it too much to say that He retires and withdraws? There is reason for believing—and the history of many a church has shown it—that a church, as well as an individual, may not only grieve and quench the Spirit, but may commit against Him the sin which practically has no forgiveness. Certain churches, that a century ago deliberately expelled the gracious influences that went with George Whitefield's ministry, and refused to receive the reviving power that attended his preaching, have to this day remained under the curse of spiritual barrenness and deadness. And others have never recovered themselves out of the snares of the devil into which they willingly surrendered themselves, while not a few, for sins of like character, have been removed out of their place.

On the other hand, what grand results have followed the choice of thoroughly spiritual men for church offices!

The selection of these seven deacons was throughout a most godly proceeding. The suggestion of the apostles, as to the sort of men to be chosen, met unanimous response: "The saying pleased the whole multitude." The first man elected was Stephen, of whom it is expressly said that he was a man "full of faith and of the Holy Ghost," and Philip was the second. About these two men how much of the glorious history of this book revolves! Stephen was the first martyr of the apostolic church, and Philip the first of its lay evangelists. Those two men, originally set apart for a purely temporal office, have probably influenced the spiritual life and history of the church of Christ more than any other two men of the apostolic age, if we except Paul and Peter, James and John, Barnabas and Apollos. To Stephen's martyrdom we must probably trace the first impressions made upon Saul of Tarsus. Before he met Jesus in the way, and saw His glorified face, he had already seen its glory reflected in the shining face of that angelic martyr. And Philip, though a mere "layman," was the instrument chosen of the Holy Ghost to confer pentecostal blessing on Samaria, and through the eunuch, introduce the gospel into Ethiopia; while in his own person he carried the gospel even to Cesarea, and prepared the way for Peter to unlock the kingdom to the Romans![30]

Not without immense and intense significance is it recorded that the "saying" of the apostles, which so emphasized the spiritual character of church officers, "pleased the whole multitude" of believers. They were of one mind as to the style of men to be chosen, though it was not for the apostolate, but only for the diaconate—to take care of the temporal wants of widows and orphans. They must be of honest repute, to be trusted for their *integrity*, and of wisdom, to be trusted for their *sagacity*; but they must above all be full of the Holy Ghost, to be trusted for their *spirituality*.

"Them that honor me I will honor," saith God. Is it without design that, immediately after this election, it is also written that "the Word of God increased"; that "the number of the disciples multiplied in Jerusalem greatly"; that "a great company of the priests were obedient to the faith"; and that "Stephen, full of faith and power, did great wonders and miracles among the people"?[31]

There may appear to be no link joining these parts of the narrative, but the connection is vital. Give to the Spirit, as chief Administrator, men after His own mind to carry out His divine policy, and you give the head competent and willing hands and feet to do His bidding. He can thus work unhindered. Let any church prayerfully choose officers preeminently from a sense of spiritual fitness—not because they have honest report and worldly wisdom, wealth, culture, and social standing; but first of all because they are men of God, and such men of God as are fit, first to perceive and receive, and then to carry out the mind of the Holy Spirit— and similar results are bound to follow; because the laws of the kingdom are more unchanging than the laws of the Medes and Persians. Prosperity will follow—not, indeed, of a worldly sort, which often brings leanness of soul—but the increased power of the Word and the increased multitude of believers.

The exact phraseology employed in this Scripture narrative is noteworthy: "The Word of God increased"—as though in such men as the seven deacons there were somehow a new gospel of God, a new epistle of the Holy Ghost! And again— let us observe the exact phrase—"The number of the disciples *multiplied* greatly." Hitherto the word was "*added*," but now the progression is no longer arithmetical, but geometrical; not by additions, but multiplications! And it is a great company of *priests* that become obedient to the faith! The church gave Holy Ghost *deacons* and got converted *priests*.

What a striking narrative of the acts of the Holy Ghost, who, godlike in grace, does "exceeding abundantly above all that we ask or think"! Men were chosen to serve tables—to do common things; but they were found doing uncommon things—working signs and wonders among the people; dispensing not only rations of food and supplies for the body, but spiritual gifts and graces as well. In making provision to have Holy Ghost men caring for poor widows, how little did the church foresee the resistless wisdom and spirit with which Stephen and Philip were to administer the Word, and how the spirit of prophecy was to descend even upon the four virgin daughters of Philip! The disciples chose Holy Ghost deacons, and got Holy Ghost martyrs and evangelists; they selected men to serve tables, and one of them bore a face that shone as the face of an angel, and amid a shower of stones he fell asleep, like his Master, with a prayer for his murderers on his lips. The last glimpse we get of Stephen, like the first, is this: "He, being full of the Holy Ghost, looked up steadfastly into heaven, and saw the glory of God, and Jesus standing on the right hand of God."[32]

His last charge against his persecutors and stoners was, "Ye do always resist the Holy Ghost." Stephen was himself so full of the Holy Spirit that in resisting him they resisted the Spirit, and in casting stones at him they were hurling insult and injury against that invisible Administrator of the church, who dwelt in him and gave him utterance.

Such, then, is our next step in this grand series of teachings as to the acts of the Holy Ghost. We call it, for lack of any better term, the Ministry of the Spirit, because it shows us how, through all those who serve in His name, He is really administering; and that, therefore, so far as, from pastor down to sexton, the church gives position and authority to ungodly or unspiritual men, the result is to hinder and hamper the ministry of the Spirit.

---

28. Acts 6:3.
29. 1 Cor. 2:8, 14.
30. Acts 8:40.
31. Acts 6:7-8.
32. Acts 7:55.

6

The Love and Leading of the Spirit

IN THESE ACTS OF the Holy Ghost we now meet quite a new and marvelous revelation of the modes of His activity. We trace His twofold operation: first working upon the *multitude*, and secondly upon the *individual*. The former lays but a new emphasis upon what was previously exemplified; but the latter is an entirely new revealing of His secret mystery of working.

When the first persecution—of which Stephen's death by stoning was the awful signal—drove believers out of Jerusalem and scattered them abroad, Philip went down to Samaria and bore witness to Christ, and so the first missionary work in the regions beyond Judea was begun by the apostolic church, following the order of our Lord's farewell message: "Ye shall be witnesses unto me both in Jerusalem, and in all Judea, *and in Samaria.*"[33]

Philip's preaching was singularly blessed. His full position as the pioneer evangelist has never been appreciated. All Samaria seems to have been his field of labor; and after his interview with the eunuch of Ethiopia he "was found at Azotus, and passing through he preached in all the cities till he came to Cesarea,"[34] where, as we have seen, he probably laid the basis upon which Peter built when he visited the palace of the Caesars in that city of the centurion. And he not only preached over this wide circuit, but he wrought miracles, healing the lame and palsied and many possessed with demons. Tidings reached Jerusalem of this wonder-working of God in Samaria, and Peter and John were sent down to visit the new converts; and as they prayed and laid hands on them a Samaritan Pentecost followed, like unto that first outpouring in the sacred city. This is significant as marking a distinct stage in the development of this history of the acts of the Holy Ghost; for it is the first time that He came in power upon any believers, outside of Jerusalem and Judea.

The Holy Spirit here *broke for the first time the caste lines and limits of exclusion.* The Jews, despising the Samaritans as a hybrid race, a mongrel stock, which mixed the true faith with their heathen idolatries, had with them "no dealings." To show a lost traveler his way, or point a thirsty pilgrim to a water-spring, was more than the ordinary Jew would do for one of Samaria. Yet God used persecution to insure *contact;* through contact the Spirit wrought *conversion,* and so humbled the aristocratic Jew by showing Himself as ready to gather out a people for His name from these despised outcasts as from the elect nation itself that made them outcasts—yes, and equally ready to pour out His fullness at Ahab's capital as at David's metropolis.

After Peter and John had returned to Jerusalem we have on record a new lesson on the administration of the Holy Spirit, most instructive and inspiring. We have seen Him, from the day of Pentecost on, moving on *multitudes*; we now trace His motions in the *individual*, and see Him in His individual dealing and leading—observing how He guides *one believer* and leads *one inquirer*.

Hitherto we have had no distinct glimpse of such individualism; but, in this eighth chapter, we find constant traces of the Spirit's love for one soul, and of His watchful care over one disciple. An angel bids Philip go toward the south, unto the way that leads from Jerusalem toward Gaza. This was not like the closely populated district where he had been laboring, but a desert road. But there is a solitary inquirer traveling that way, and the Holy Spirit sends the evangelist on a long and apparently useless journey simply to meet and guide that one soul. The eunuch of Ethiopia, treasurer of Candace the queen, is returning homeward, and searching the prophecy of Isaiah about the Messiah, of whom, no doubt, he had heard at Jerusalem.

And thus, for the first time in the acts of the Holy

Ghost, we see the Spirit no longer moving upon the multitude, but condescending to become the personal guide of one believer, and through him of one inquirer: "THE SPIRIT SAID UNTO PHILIP, Go near, and join thyself to this chariot." The evangelist, like his Lord, is led up of the Spirit into the wilderness, not, indeed, to be tempted, but to guide a seeking soul to salvation. The Spirit holds direct communication with this deacon and preacher, and speaks to him, bidding him to go and teach this man the way of life.

This lesson is too precious to be lightly passed over. Here is the Creator Spirit seen moving, not upon the abyss of waters, to develop life in a new world, but moving upon two human hearts: on one that he may search the Scriptures so as to find their testimony concerning the Christ; on the other that he may guide and help such a seeker with the light of his own experience. Thus, the Holy Spirit is seen in His individual "acts"—His love for the individual soul. He deigns to *lead two men into contact.* Christ "loved the world," "loved the church," but not less "loved *me,* and gave himself for *me*"; so the Spirit loves and leads the individual soul, expending all the divine energy of His power and wisdom upon one inquirer and one teacher. He has been doing just such individual work ever since, and will continue such work till the end of the age.

Nor does this eighth chapter close until we have

one more glimpse of this individual dealing. For when the eunuch, believing, had received baptism at the hands of the evangelist, it is added:

"THE SPIRIT OF THE LORD CAUGHT AWAY PHILIP."

The obvious impression is that of a supernatural "rapture." The errand of the Spirit was accomplished, and He removed the messenger, and he was found at Azotus, miles distant.[35] Not only did the Holy Spirit condescend to bring these two men together, but as soon as the special service to which Philip was called was fulfilled, He caught him up and bore him away to another quarter. We are reminded of that journey taken by Christ from the Galilean lake to those same coasts of Cesarea, taken apparently for the sole purpose of imparting blessing to that needy woman of Canaan whose daughter was grievously vexed with a demon;[36] for on the entire journey to and fro, no other miracle of Christ is recorded, no other act done.

The narrative of Saul's conversion follows. Here the Lord Jesus in His proper person appears very conspicuous, as in the gospel narratives, but as in *no other place* in this book of the Acts of the Holy Ghost. For the time we lose sight of the Spirit, as though the Lord Himself had returned, and the Paraclete was no longer so needful to the disciple. It is the Lord Jesus Himself who appears in a vision both to Saul and to Ananias.

There is a special reason. Christ is now *calling a new*

apostle, and the call must be direct and personal; for one fundamental qualification of an apostle was that he had "seen the Lord" after He was risen, and could witness, from personal knowledge, to His resurrection. But be it noticed that before the narrative concludes, the Holy Spirit again comes to the front; for we are told that all this vision of the Lord Jesus in the way, and the mission on which Ananias was sent, were in order that this newly converted persecutor might "be filled with the Holy Ghost."[37] Even Christ, though He may appear in person to call this new apostle and give him his commission, leaves the work of his regeneration and qualification to be carried on and completed by the Spirit. And it is significantly added that "immediately there fell from his eyes as it had been scales."[38] The vision of Christ and baptism unto Christ sufficed not to make a disciple and apostle, without the Spirit's baptism, anointing, and teaching.[39] There was need of His illumination, that all scales might be removed and the spiritual vision be clarified. And from this time forth, like his Master before him, Saul was to be led of the Spirit. In the power of the Spirit he was to keep in union and communion with the risen Redeemer, and bear witness to His resurrection; to undertake those first mission tours; to gather converts and organize them into churches; to write inspired epistles, and in his own holy living furnish a still more striking epistle of God.

If this chapter seems in its opening verses to bring the risen Christ into more prominence than the Paraclete, we shall find further on a reference to the Spirit so unique and comprehensive that it might have furnished the name for this whole discussion, and may well stand for the motto of the entire book we are studying. We give the most approved reading as well as the common version:

"Then had the churches rest throughout all Judea and Galilee and Samaria, and were edified; and walking in the fear of the Lord, and in the *comfort of the Holy Ghost*, were multiplied."[40]

"Then had the church rest,. . .being built up; and, walking in the fear of the Lord and in the *paraclesis of the Holy Spirit*, was multiplied."

The important phrase which, in either reading, is the central feature in this description of the church's true growth and its conditions, is that which we have italicized: "In the Comfort," or "Paraclesis, of the Holy Spirit." It contains that word paraclesis which, like that mysterious name paracletos to which it exactly corresponds, is untranslatable. It really includes *all the work of the Paraclete*, whether in the church or the world: His demonstration of the truth even to sinners, His illumination of the mind and heart of saints, His regeneration and sanctification of the whole man, His edification of the body of Christ—in a word, His *entire administration of the whole church life and church work*. All this is embraced in this word "paraclesis," rendered "comfort," as its fellow-word is rendered "comforter"; but how inadequately in either case, since but a small part of the acts of the Holy Ghost can be represented by what we mean by "comfort," though it be true that, when that word was first used by the translators of King James's version, centuries ago, it meant far more than now!

Upon this verse and this phrase we have the less need now to tarry because the whole of this humble treatise which we are now writing is in fact devoted to its explication and application. But is it not already but too evident that the church of our day has little or no conception of the pricelessness of blessing involved in this paraclesis of the Spirit? What if once more this lesson could be learned? What "rest" would the church have from internal dissension and division, from heresy and schism! What edification, "being built up" on the most holy faith! What holy "walking in the fear of the Lord," what rapid multiplication, and what world-wide evangelization! There is not an evil now cursing or threatening our church life which this "comfort of the Holy Ghost" would not remedy and perhaps remove.

33.   Acts 1:8.
34.   Acts 8:40.
35.   Acts 8:39-40.
36.   Matt. 15:21.

37.   Acts 9:17.
38.   Acts 9:18.
39.   Acts 22:16.
40.   Acts 9:31.

7

The Forecast and Foretaste of the Spirit

THE NEW PENTECOST OF Cesarea, which next confronts us in the acts of the Holy Ghost, has an apparent *prophetic* bearing, which impresses us more and more as we study it. In this tenth chapter of this book there is an unveiling of the Spirit and His work, so far in advance of all hitherto revealed or exhibited that we cannot but see in it at least a possible and probable forecast and foretaste of things to come.

This is the record of the first outpouring of the Spirit, outside of Judea and Samaria, and touching the "uttermost part of the earth," for it came upon a representative *Roman* gathering.

The steps of preparation are significant. Philip had gone as far as Cesarea, preaching the Word— probably the pioneer evangelist at this city of Caesar. Saul, after his conversion, and escape from Damascus, and visit to Jerusalem, was brought down to Cesarea on his way to Tarsus. It would be unlike this converted persecutor not to have borne his testimony also to Christ and his salvation in this home of the Roman centurion.

Certain it is that the next step is now reached in *Peter's visit to Cesarea.* And—what is the vital matter— it is all *the work of the Spirit.* As in the case of Philip and the eunuch, God's angel, the human messenger, and the Holy Spirit, are seen acting in cooperation, and the parallel is too close to have been accidental or incidental. The angel of the Lord "spake to Philip," and now to Cornelius; the Spirit said unto Philip, "Go near," and now again to Peter, "Go with them." In fact, upon this basis of the double guidance of angel and Holy Spirit, these two narratives are built. They are like twin witnesses, each confirming the other, and both teaching one lesson.

Here again we observe the *personality* of the Spirit, guarded. We read of a "voice" that thrice spake; but further on a notable change takes place in the language used. It might easily have been the same, and the record might have read that "while Peter thought on the vision, a *voice* said unto him";[41] but the design is manifestly to bring to the front and keep at the front the acts of the Holy Ghost, as a *person,* and so it is written:

". . .THE SPIRIT SAID UNTO HIM, Behold, three men seek thee. Arise therefore, and get thee down, and go with them, doubting nothing: FOR I HAVE SENT THEM."[42]

No "angel" or "voice" or "vision" or "influence

from above" uses such terms. A divine Being is speaking. And Peter at once goes to the men, prepared to heed their summons as the call of the Holy Spirit. Whether or not divine commissions are yet executed by vision, voice, or angel, that same Spirit abides with us forever, for He is not among the transient gifts of God.

The effect of this communication from the Spirit is seen in Peter's whole course and attitude. Without delay he went to Cesarea as the commissioned messenger of the Holy Ghost. His authority was not original, but derived, and when Cornelius met him with worshipful homage, he naturally said, "Stand up; I myself also am a man."[43] How could he indulge, or even *have*, any sense of his own importance, with mind and memory charged with the recent manifestation of the Spirit's presence and his own reception of a divine commission! He felt, like many another messenger of the Most High, that another Presence was in that place of assembly, in comparison with which he was insignificant.

Brief as the discourse was, Peter could not introduce it without referring to the Holy Spirit as constituting the anointing power which made Jesus Himself so mighty in word and deed.[44]

But the grand verse of this chapter is this: "While Peter yet spake these words, THE HOLY GHOST FELL ON ALL THEM WHICH HEARD THE WORD."[45] And with this we should place, side by side, the corresponding verse in the next chapter: "AS I BEGAN TO SPEAK, THE HOLY GHOST FELL ON THEM, AS ON US AT THE BEGINNING."[46]

Combining these two testimonies to one and the same event, we get this comprehensive statement: "While Peter yet spake, and as he began to speak, the Holy Ghost fell on all them which heard the Word, being poured out as on the disciples at the beginning"—from which we learn three or four lessons:

1. Peter's discourse was *broken off* in its incompleteness.
2. The Holy Spirit fell on *Gentile hearers* as before on Jewish.
3. The outpouring was, for the first time, on *all that heard*;
4. And, also for the first time, it was *previous to baptism*.

At all four points these lessons are in advance of any hitherto learned. Peter's address was apparently arrested in the midst of its delivery. We may imagine how his mind would naturally have been occupied on the journey from Joppa to Cesarea. The gospel was now to be first formally proclaimed to the Romans in the very palace of the Caesars, and to "Caesar's household"; and he, the typical Jew, was to open to them the "door of faith." With such notice of his errand served beforehand, and knowing the important commission he was to discharge, Peter

would have been more or less than human had he
not in the interval between the vision and the sermon been meditating on the message he was to
deliver. The address betrays this forethought, and
suggests a careful ordering of thought whose pre-
sentation was only *begun* when further utterance
was made so strangely unnecessary. Yet enough had
been said for the Spirit to *make saving use of it*—Christ
being held up as the anointed, crucified, risen
Saviour, witnessed to by prophets, testified to by
believers; and the essence of the whole gospel
having been compressed and expressed in one brief
sentence: "Through his name whosoever believeth
in him shall receive remission of sins."[47] That was
enough—the Spirit could now work His saving
change in the hearts of the hearers; and at once,
while Peter yet spake the words of salvation, the
Spirit of God, as with a divine impatience, set aside
both messenger and message, and that whole
audience received not only the new birth, but the
new baptism, simultaneously.

Again, here was a new Pentecost, similar to that at
Jerusalem, and accompanied by similar signs, even to
the gift of tongues. The six brethren who came with
Peter from Joppa, with astonishment beheld an
unprecedented thing: *no distinction made between the circumcision and the uncircumcision*, even in that most
precious gift of the Spirit! Hitherto all such bestowments of grace had been upon the circumcised and

the baptized; but now upon those who had known neither of these separating rites. The Holy Spirit thus broke through all caste lines, all old restraints of ritual, and even the sacramental limits so conspicuous in the church of the New Testament. We can imagine something of the startling emphasis of Peter's question: "Can any man forbid water, that these should not be baptized, *which have received the Holy Ghost as well as we?*"[48] Think of it!—a Jew constrained to confess that God's Spirit had been actually poured out in all His fullness on Gentiles—in advance of circumcision and baptism!

And yet again, we notice that the Spirit fell on *all that heard the Word.* It would seem that these hearers, however *prepared*, were not previously *converted*; for the angel, when be bade Cornelius send for Peter, said, "He shall tell thee what thou oughtest to do,"[49] or, as more fully expressed by Peter, "words, whereby thou and all thy house shall be saved."[50] The outpouring at Jerusalem had been upon *baptized believers* only, and through their witness the Spirit reached out to the unsaved. He became the anointing power to *believers* first, and through them the convicting and converting power to *unbelievers*; and this seems to be the law of His activity through this whole dispensation.

What, then, can be the significance of this exceptional outpouring on unbaptized and unbelieving hearers, if it be not a type—a forecast and foretaste of things to come? Peter did not declare, of the pentecostal outpouring at Jerusalem, that it *fulfilled* the prophecy of Joel which explained its nature; for Joel predicted an outpouring *"upon all flesh"*—a latter rain more copiously abundant, which should come down in converting power upon all that hear. If this be, as we believe, the true key both to the prophecy and the history, we have a grand explanation of the mystery of these two pentecostal scenes: the former is the key to the acts of the Holy Ghost in this dispensation, or age of witness and out gathering, when He comes only upon His chosen witnessbearers; the latter is the key to the coming age, when His operations shall be so widened that He shall descend upon "all flesh," and "all flesh shall see the salvation of God."

This impression is strengthened by the language of Peter, who emphasizes the fact, saying: "God gave them the like gift as he did unto us, who believed,"[51] as though this outpouring was on those who had not hitherto believed; as also is made emphatic by the fact that in such bestowment of the Spirit God had "also to the Gentiles granted repentance unto life."

In the eleventh chapter of the Acts we have Peter, after his return to Jerusalem rehearsing the housetop vision, with the subsequent steps that led him to Cornelius's palace, without essential addition or modification. Though there is little that is new, repetition gives emphasis to the *personal guidance* of the Spirit, which is the grand truth here taught, leading us also to expect plain indications of duty whenever we are truly surrendered to the Lord for service.

The language uniformly used of the Spirit's baptism in all these instances suggests *affusion* or *effusion*, and seems to have been typified by the anointing with oil. The exact words are noticeable: first the quotation from Joel: "I will *pour out* of my Spirit"; then Peter's own words: "He hath *shed forth this*";[52] then, in this later narrative: "The Holy Ghost *fell on* them. . .Then remembered I the word of the Lord,. . . Ye shall be *baptized* with the Holy Ghost."[53] If such language carries to a common and candid mind any impression, it is that when the Spirit is poured out, shed forth, or falls upon men, *that* is His baptism. And those who hold immersion to be the only legitimate *water* baptism must concede that the baptism of the *Spirit* is described in the Scriptures in the terms of affusion or pouring.

In these acts of the Holy Ghost much is properly traceable to His working which is not actually *traced* to Him. Thus, also, in the Book of Esther, God's hand is seen where His name is not found. Seemingly there is a "lot cast into the lap"; really "the whole disposing thereof is of the Lord."

The great number of believers at Antioch was due to the ministry of the Spirit. It is said, "*The hand of the*

Lord was with them,"[54] and this marked expression may be the equivalent here of the Spirit's power as it appears to be, when used of the forerunner of Christ, who from birth was peculiarly filled with the Holy Ghost.[55] Grand metaphor indeed to express the active operation of the Spirit!—THE HAND OF THE LORD. The Word of God is the sword of the Spirit, and a sword needs a hand to grasp, hold, and wield it; the truth of God is a hammer, and needs a hand to give effectiveness to its blows. If vessels are to be molded and fitted for service, a hand must do the shaping and filling and carrying. Surely wherever the gospel is triumphant it is the Holy Spirit who is the hand of the Lord, breaking hard hearts with His hammer, piercing to the dividing asunder of soul and spirit with His sword, molding vessels unto honor for the Master's use upon His potter's wheel.

In the brief portrait of Barnabas, goodness and faith are but the handmaids of a central quality and characteristic: he was "full of the Holy Ghost." And because of this "much people was *added unto the Lord.*" Here again we meet that curious and unique word "added," or the phrase, "added to the Lord."[56]

Again we catch a glimpse of the Spirit, and this time in a new phase—acting upon a disciple prophetically, as when, by the Spirit, Agabus prophesied of the coming dearth.[57]

But more important still is that twelfth chapter,

which, without any direct mention of the Spirit, exhibits His working in bringing about what our Lord calls the *symphony of prayer*.[58]

Peter is in prison awaiting execution, and ceaseless prayer is made for Him by the church. The prayer prevails; and the angel of the Lord by night opens the doors, and loosens the fetters of the apostle, and makes the iron gate to open of its own accord. We have here an example of the acts of the Holy Ghost in *uniting believers in supplication*. Only He can, in the soul of the individual believer, awaken the "unutterable groanings" after God and holiness; and only He can bring praying believers into sympathy and symphony in united prayer. That promise of power as dependent on agreement must not be applied to mere voluntary and arbitrary agreement of disciples *with one another*; it implies, first of all, higher unity *with* and *in* the Spirit. Symphony, which is the result of musical accord and concord, is neither arbitrary nor accidental; it obeys the law of the chord and is awakened by the intelligent hand which *touches only such keys* as are in harmony. It is therefore only when believing, praying souls are led by the Spirit into true accord, that the Lord's promise applies; then, although they may be strangers to one another, they may be led into such fellowship through the Spirit as to pray at the same time for the same object. The church is like some grand instrument on whose keys the divine Artist lays His hand, and so makes united prayers to sound, like chords of music, in God's ear. And how far great results are traceable to the often unconscious unity of praying souls will be divulged only on that day when the books are opened.

---

41.   Acts 10:13, 15.
42.   Acts 10:19, 20.
43.   Acts 10:26.
44.   Acts 10:38.
45.   Acts 10:44.
46.   Acts 11:15.
47.   Acts 10:43.
48.   Acts 10:47.
49.   Acts 10:6.
50.   Acts 11:14.
51.   Acts 11:17-18.
52.   Acts 2:33.
53.   Acts 11:15-16.
54.   Acts 11:21.
55.   Luke 1:66.
56.   Acts 11:24. Cf. 2:41, 47; 5:14.
57.   Acts 11:28.
58.   Matt. 18:19.

8

The Calling and Sending of the Spirit

THE BIRTH-HOUR OF early missions to the Gentiles, considered as an organized effort, was reached when from Antioch, Barnabas and Saul took their departure.[59]

This thirteenth chapter of the Acts must be set side by side with Matthew 9:37-38. There we have the *precept* and *principle*: "Pray ye therefore the Lord of the harvest, that he would thrust forth laborers into his harvest." Here we have the *practice* and *example*: a praying church and the divine calling out and sending forth of the workers. No doubt this church, so largely gathered from the Gentiles, would be more likely to be peculiarly drawn out in sympathetic intercession for the Gentiles. And here we see the way in which the Lord supplies workers when the church offers believing prayers:

"THE HOLY GHOST SAID, SEPARATE ME BARNABAS AND SAUL FOR THE WORK WHEREUNTO I HAVE CALLED THEM. . .SO THEY, BEING SENT FORTH BY THE HOLY GHOST, DEPARTED."

How could the personality and activity of the Holy Spirit in the affairs of the church be more plainly, grandly taught and shown! Only a person *speaks, calls, calls by name, sends forth.* The Spirit designates the very men He has chosen, and sends them forth.

In fact, there is a new exhibition of the Spirit's authority in this crisis of affairs: "So they, being *sent forth* by the Holy Ghost." The Holy Spirit has His *"apostles,"* for the word "apostle," or "missionary," means one who is sent forth—one word being from the Greek, the other from the Latin. Hitherto the term "apostle" has had a specific meaning and been limited to the men chosen by Christ personally or in Christ's name. But, turning to the next chapter, we read, "Which when the *apostles, Barnabas* and *Paul,* heard," etc.[60] The Spirit of God gives apostolic authority and sends forth whom He will as an apostle of the Holy Ghost.

The important thought, however, is that there are certain men, Barnabas and Saul, whom He has chosen, and would have separated unto Himself. Behind all the action of the Antiochan church, behold the acts of the Holy Ghost—a designation, a vocation, a separation, a commission, a dismission— all of Him and expressly attributed to Him.[61]

Those who were thus called of the Spirit and sent forth by Him would, of course, be accompanied by signs of His presence and power. Saul no sooner begins his new ministry at Paphos than he gives proof of being filled with the Spirit; for he works a judicial miracle upon Elymas, the sorcerer, in the infliction of blindness—a typical miracle;[62] for this sorcerer not only closed his own eyes to the truth, but like a blind leader of the blind, would have turned away Sergius Paulus from the truth that both might fall into the ditch. And so Saul, henceforth known as Paul (the "Little"), who is to grow less in his own eyes, that the Spirit may be magnified—Saul-Paul is led of the Spirit to smite with judicial blindness him who chose both to walk in darkness and to lead others into it.

As this chapter closes we are told that "the disciples were filled with joy, and with the Holy Ghost"; the divine Person is still kept before us, and even fullness of joy is seen to be one of the results of the acts of the Holy Ghost.

The *witness* of the Spirit is now again exhibited and declared, with more emphasis and particularity than before. In the fourteenth chapter and third verse we have another example of the indirect references to the Spirit's working with which this book abounds: "The Lord *gave testimony* unto the Word of his grace." How? By the acts of the Holy Ghost. Christ had promised that, as the disciples bore witness to Him, they should find Another bearing witness with them and to them—a greater testimony confirming and sealing their own. And all through these acts of the Holy Ghost we may trace this double witness going forward; in fact, as we have seen already, there was a threefold witness—to them, with them, through them. Here His testimony is referred to in relation to its confirmation of them and their work. While they witnessed to a risen Christ, the Spirit also gave His testimony to them and to their word, by signs and wonders wrought in the power of the Spirit, and by working that greatest of all miracles, a regenerate heart. Such results of preaching are at once a *demonstration* and an *attestation*.

That the Holy Spirit's joint testimony with that of disciples is referred to in the verse now under consideration will appear to any reader who takes pains to put side by side three memorable passages of the inspired Word:[63]

John 15:26, 27	Mark 16:20	Hebrews 2:4
"The Spirit of truth. . .shall bear witness of me: and ye also shall bear witness."	"And they went forth, and preached everywhere, the Lord working with, and confirming the Word with signs following."	"God also bearing them witness, both with signs and wonders, and with divers miracles, and gifts of the Holy Ghost."

The peculiar expression in the twenty-sixth verse of this chapter, as to their sailing "to Antioch, from whence they had been *recommended to the grace of God* for the work which they fulfilled,"[64] like a similar phrase in the next chapter, may be another indirect reference to Holy Ghost guidance. What does this mean, if not that these disciples, who had been specially set apart for mission work, had been given over, committed, intrusted to the presence, guidance, power of the Holy Spirit? As this book is full of His holy administration, it is also full of that voluntary submission and surrender to His will which is the corresponding factor in all true co-work and co-witness: *enduement* and *endowment* on the one hand, *intrustment* and *commitment* on the other; these are the secrets of power in service. The Holy Spirit can administer only so far as we commit ourselves and others to His blessed rule and control; and all those who are thus by the church intrusted, and do intrust themselves to His divine "guidance and governance," will have afterward, like Paul and Barnabas, much to rehearse in the ears of the church as to what God has done with them. God the Holy Ghost acts through human instruments, and can do great things, both in opening doors of faith to unbelievers, and in confirming the work of faith in believers, if He finds instruments wholly intrusted to His keeping and using.[65]

This intrustment and commitment of ourselves to the Spirit corresponds to that aspect of saving faith which is properly called trust. As Prebendary Webb-Peploe well says, "Faith is receiving, trust is committing": one gets, the other gives; one takes the gift of eternal life from God on the basis of His Word, the other gives back the life He has given, to be kept and used by Him. This latter aspect of intrustment is well expressed by the term *yield*—"Yield yourselves unto God, as those that are alive from the dead, and your members as instruments of righteousness unto God."[66] Paul writes to Timothy, "I know whom I have believed, and am persuaded that he is able to keep that which I have committed unto him."[67] Here are the four degrees or stages of faith: *belief, persuasion, commitment, knowledge* or *assurance*.

So in our relation to the Spirit there is a double aspect: first we *receive* Him as Christ's ascension gift, then we *intrust* or *commit* ourselves to His indwelling, inworking, outworking. The former act is the opening of the heart and whole being to His blessed incoming, the latter is the giving up to His possession and power, service, and control the whole being He indwells, that He may find every member of the body, every faculty of the mind, every affection of the heart, obedient to His behests and ready to do His bidding; so that the will, itself the natural sovereign of our being—like "a man under authority," the centurion, having soldiers under command[68]—may be only the servant of the Spirit of God, saying to all subordinate powers of body and mind, "Do this," while issuing all such commands only in the Spirit's name; acknowledging the *imperium* back of itself, and all its own authority as derived.

The supreme lesson to be learned by all disciples is this cheerful and grateful and whole-hearted self-yielding to the Spirit. All His power is at the disposal of every believer who is first at His disposal. Obedience to Him means command over others: in proportion as we are subject to Him, even the demons are subject unto us in His name; He cannot transfer His power or give His glory to another; but this is not a transfer of either His power or His glory, save as the electrical battery transfers its mighty current to the medium of transmission. You become electric or magnetic if you have connection with the generators of these mysterious forces; and in proportion as the connection is complete, and you are a good "conductor," all the power resident in the battery is transmitted through you.

"They, being sent forth by the Holy Ghost, *departed;*" that is, they, being sent forth, went forth at once, implicitly surrendering themselves to His guidance. A supernatural gospel is meant to accomplish supernatural results, and needs a supernatural power behind it and its messengers. We who are the heralds of Christ need to feel that we are not only dealing with divine things, but with a divine Person; and that only as we obey Him and submit to His control and guidance can we have power.

The Rev. Dr. Skinner, of New York, used to say that nothing contributes to a mighty ministry like a "sense of the powers of the world to come." It is possible to have a very learned and accomplished ministry and a most complete machinery of church life and all external prosperity, and yet be destitute of the power of the Spirit of God; possible to have additions to the church and no conversions to the Lord; to make an easy way into the church, and yet block the true way to Christ by the idols of ecclesiasticism. There is much talk nowadays of consecration, which means mere human *resolve*, and has no conception of the Spirit taking possession, changing the whole inner temper and life, shedding abroad the love of God, and filling the temple with His glory. It is possible to have abundant labor, and yet all in the energy of the flesh, not of the Spirit. How blessed when a man is sent forth by the Spirit and departs—goes forth at His bidding, and can say, with the holy humility of Micah, "I am full of power by the Spirit of the Lord"![69]

When Barnabas and Paul had completed this first mission tour they returned to Antioch, and "when they were come, and had gathered the church together, they rehearsed all that God had done with them, and how he had opened the door of faith unto the Gentiles."[70] Then, on their way to Jerusalem, "they passed through Phenice and Samaria, declaring the conversion of the Gentiles: and they caused great joy unto all the brethren."[71] Likewise at Jerusalem "they declared all things that God had done with them.". . ."declaring what miracles and wonders God had wrought among the Gentiles by them."[72]

Men sent forth by the Holy Ghost and going forth at His bidding will always have much to tell, but not about themselves and their great achievements. If the story told by Barnabas and Paul was wonderful, not more remarkable was it than their own *humility*. See how guardedly they keep themselves out of sight: "All that *God had* done with them"; "how *he had opened* the door of faith"; "what miracles and wonders God *had wrought* by them."

Nothing is so humbling from first to last as this gospel. We receive eternal life as a gift from God, wholly dissociated from all good works of our own; and when we have the gift, He who gave it must nourish and maintain it moment by moment. We receive the Holy Spirit, and He gives—or rather becomes in us—power; and even this power will cease to be exerted the moment we become self-reliant or self-confident. This is the lesson, not of this chapter alone, but of every chapter in this book. The only hope of the believer or of the church for power in praying or preaching, living for God or laboring with God, is found in the perpetual indwelling and inworking of the Spirit. If He is loved, worshiped, adored as God; if His presence and presidency are recognized and cherished; if all is done in subordination to His authority and for His glory; if all achieved is humbly attributed to His working, He will continue to hold in the church His seat, and make it the true body of Christ where

every member moves in obedience to its divine
Head.

---

59. Acts 13:1-5.
60. Acts 14:14.
61. Cf. *New Acts of the Apostles* (by the writer), part 2, chap. 1.
62. Acts 13:9-12.
63. Cf. also Acts 15:8: "God. . .bare them witness, giving them
     the Holy Ghost," etc.
64. Acts 15:40.
65. Acts 14:27; 15:3, 4, 12.
66. Rom. 6:13.
67. 2 Tim. 1:12.
68. Matt. 8:9.
69. Mic. 3:8.
70. Acts 14:27.
71. Acts 15:3.
72. Acts 15:4, 12.

9

The Counsel and Approval of the Spirit

WE REACH NOW THE heart of this fifth Gospel, the acts of the Holy Ghost. The fifteenth chapter, which is very nearly central in this narrative, affords a singularly clear exhibition of His working and co-working in the church, and supplies both a pivotal center for His activities, and a focal center of convergence where the revelations of His condescending love and grace meet in a point of intense glory.

In the course of this narrative words are written which for startling impressiveness are elsewhere, even in this book of surprises, unequaled, and which at first seem irreverent:

"IT SEEMED GOOD TO THE HOLY GHOST, AND TO US."[73]

This is the formal announcement of the conclusions and decisions of that first church council at Jerusalem. Apostles and elders have been in conference over certain troublesome and somewhat vexatious questions of ceremonialism, which verge closely upon the domain of Christian ethics. And now, as they draw up their "deliverance," and formally issue letters conveying their final verdict, they boldly treat the Holy Spirit *as one of their number*— a fellow-counselor, who unites with them in the announcement of a joint conclusion; as though He, the Spirit of God, had sat with them in their deliberations, had with them counseled as chief adviser, and now unites with them in this deliverance, sealing their conclusions with His approval. As no such language, or anything closely approaching it, occurs elsewhere in the Word of God, its emphasis cannot be mistaken. In the earlier part of this letter to the Gentile converts, the disciples, convened at Jerusalem, had said, "It seemed good *unto us*, being assembled with one accord, to send chosen men unto you,"[74] and this is the natural language of brethren who have been in session deliberating over common questions. But, as though One who was at the same time the presiding officer and chief counselor should be mentioned by name, they now, as they approach the very heart of their message to Gentile churches, add, "It seemed good *to the HOLY GHOST, and to us.*" There is no resisting the implication that He had been assembled with them and was with them of one accord.

In this exalted truth we seem to reach the apex of the teaching of this book. In the fifth chapter we saw the Spirit's presence and presidency exhibited in the church, so that back of Peter, as the apparent head,

He stood as the real Administrator of affairs. Then in the sixth chapter we saw Him, as the Archbishop and Primate of the whole church, controlling all subordinate offices so that they shall be filled only by men who are first filled with the Spirit and prepared to cooperate with Him and be subordinate to Him. Then in the eighth and ninth chapters we traced His individual dealing and leading, bringing chosen workmen and inquiring souls together. Again in the thirteenth chapter we have seen Him choosing and calling by name, separating and sending forth the first two missionaries to regions beyond. And now we reach a still loftier level, where He is seen not only occupying the higher seat of sovereignty, but condescending to the lowlier seat of fellow-counselor.

Here is a lesson for all ages on the *true character of church councils.* What we call a "court of Jesus Christ" has too often been more like an assembly of unbelievers, if not like a "synagogue of Satan." When in church meetings for business—even business so sacred as the election of a pastor—and when, in those higher courts where the wider interests of the churches are adjusted, we find subtlety and diplomacy, worldly policy and temporizing expediency, even downright deception and dishonesty, practised; when we find a party spirit existing, and warring factions, hot with controversy, waging ecclesiastical warfare, and politicians pulling wires and pursuing personal and selfish schemes; when we hear little prayer or praise, and much noise and confusion and clamor of excited, if not angry, debate, and occasionally witness scenes of uproar that would disgrace a political caucus—we have been compelled to stop and ask, IS THIS A COURT OF CHRIST? IS THE HOLY GHOST HERE? Is this the SEE of a divine Archbishop, or is it the "seat of Satan"?

What a radical revolution would take place in all church assemblies if the sense of the Spirit's presence were actually felt, and if everything were said and done as in His presence! We have known church meetings, nominally called for transaction of the Lord's special business, and opened with a solemn invocation of the presence and guidance of the Spirit of God, which had been "packed" by design with parties pledged to a certain course of action, and where any opposition to such predetermined policy was met with riotous demonstration and violent disturbance; or, in other cases, church courts conducted, indeed, with more apparent deference to the decencies of external order, but where there was an underhand conspiracy quietly to carry out some subtle scheme and defeat all opposition, however sincere and reasonable. If such conduct is not a practical *unseating* of the Holy Spirit, what can be?

On the contrary, we could mention by name at least one church of Christ where for a score of years the sense of the Spirit's presence has been habitually and sedulously cultivated; where everything is done as unto the Lord and before Him; where disciples tread softly, as in the unseen Presence; where nothing would be done or countenanced which was felt to be out of harmony with His mind or not in positive accord with His leading; where clamor and confusion would be deemed an insult to His majestic dignity, and all insubordination an assault upon His rightful sovereignty; where His mind is first of all inquired after and waited for, as an inquirer awaits the response of an oracle before taking a step at a crisis; where a certain *atmosphere* prevails which is fragrant with His presence and inspiring with His vitality. Of the conclusions reached by such a body of disciples it might be even now no irreverence, were it written, "*It seemed good to the Holy Ghost, and to us.*"

Perhaps no one lesson among all those taught in this book is designed to leave a more deep and lasting impression. The Holy Spirit's *acts must be recognized* if they are to be real and effective and constant. Here, as in so many other cases, the law is, "According to your faith be it unto you." This is a fact revealed only to faith, possible only to faith. His presence is not one to be seen, heard, felt, or known by bodily organs or senses, but by the spirit that is in fellow-ship with Him. When and where He is revered, recognized, and treated as actually present and presiding, leading and teaching, guiding and governing, He actually is exercising all His blessed offices of administration. Where His counsel is sought and waited for in faith, and where every step is taken as under His eye and obedient to His glance, He actually does lead and control. And it is no irreverence to say of any conclusion so reached, "It seemed good"; not only "to us," but "to the Holy Ghost." But, where He is treated with neglect as though not present, or with contempt as though unworthy of worshipful reverence and obedience, He is grieved and quenched, and virtually forsakes His seat in the church and leaves it to the usurper, the world, and the prince of this world, whose presence and guidance are practically preferred.

This one phrase needs but to be devoutly studied and its lesson thoroughly learned, to introduce into our whole church administration a new principle of life and power unknown since apostolic days; and make our church courts—instead of burrowing places for ecclesiastical foxes, and nests for intriguers who may be "wise as serpents," but who, alas! are not quite as "harmless as doves"—as holy and sacred as the house of God, as attractive and glorious as the gate of heaven.

One voice and pen that left blessed testimony to the church on this subject have given their last contribution to the great theme.[75] For more than twenty years he quietly but earnestly devoted his noble powers to the study and advocacy of the Holy Spirit's administration in the church; and he has left behind four books which together constitute a complete witness on this subject—we might almost say, a complete literature of the theme. In *The Ministry of the Spirit* he treats the manifold offices of the Spirit and the modes of His working; in *The Holy Spirit and Missions* he gives us a practical commentary on the thirteenth chapter of the Acts, in which the Holy Ghost appears, choosing and sending forth the first missionaries; in *How Christ Came to Church*, founded on a dream of the Master's presence in the sanctuary, he works out the problem of conforming church life to the pattern left by the Spirit on the pages of the Acts, and making real His actual presidency; and in the *Coronation Hymnal* he sought to furnish a vehicle for spiritual song appropriate to the uses of the Spirit in the service of praise, and to that "speaking among ourselves, and teaching and admonishing one another in psalms and hymns and spiritual songs," which is expressly enjoined in the Pauline Epistles.[76]

In all the blessed ministry of Dr. Gordon no testimony is to be found that is a more valuable legacy to the church than this witness to the Spirit. It was a perpetual "burden" on his mind and heart, like those of the prophets of old; and he felt that he must speak. But, best of all, he actually reduced the theory of the Spirit's administration largely to practice. For a quarter of a century he wrought, patiently teaching and preaching the doctrine of the Holy Ghost, praying for Holy Ghost power to do a higher will than his own, gradually eliminating from the church of which he was pastor the secular elements which had found their way into its working, until it presented the unique spectacle of an apostolic church, conducted by consecrated men, controlled by scriptural principles and encouraging scriptural practices; having its service of song wholly in the hands of devout leaders, its moneys all raised by voluntary offerings, prayer magnified, the Spirit honored, and mission enterprises at home and abroad so cordially sustained, that this church became the leader of a whole denomination, and a standing proof that, even in these degenerate days, the Spirit of God may be found holding His seat in the midst of His people, recognized and obeyed and honored as the presiding Power, and working His wonders of conversion and consecration, enduement and service, somewhat as of old.

Nor is this church absolutely solitary. While in Bristol, England, I visited the chapel where the body of brethren assemble, gathered under the ministry of George Muller. A half-century ago he sat down with a few disciples about the Lord's table for the distinct purpose of forming an apostolic church, in which the scriptural pattern was to be appealed to as the sole guide, and the Holy Spirit to be recognized as the sole Administrator. That little flock has increased until it has become, not two bands, but many. But during all these years there has been no departure from the model then chosen. Secular practices and methods have been kept out, and a spiritual method has been resolutely adhered to; so that the only party who administers it in any proper sense is the Spirit of God, who gives unmistakable signs of His own, of His holy presence and power continually.

It fell to the writer to be present at a prayer service in this well-known chapel in Bristol, where some three hundred persons were gathered. From the entrance into the room one impression was vivid: an invisible Presence fills this place, and so manifestly presides that no human conductor seems necessary. The exercises were spontaneous and purely voluntary; brethren offered prayer, praise, admonition, or exhortation, as they felt moved, without any indications of a program or prearrangement. Yet all was harmonious and consistent. It seemed like a sudden translation backward into the apostolic days. And it is to be noticed that this body of disciples moves in everything together. While other churches so multiply organizations within or without the church that our ecclesiastical system bids fair to become a vast, cumbrous, complex piece of machinery, and threatens to divide young and old, men and women, into separate societies; in this church of Christ all unite in any work done for the Master.

Nothing is further from the purpose of the writer than to make any invidious comparisons, or hold up to undue prominence and praise any one or more church organizations. But there is a peril that besets us which is of the gravest character. While the teaching of this inspired Book is unmistakable, it is treated as an impracticable theory, and easily dismissed as a dream of the past that the present age of church history cannot be expected to realize. Yet God has in some few instances proved in this degenerate day that there is nothing unattainable in the apostolic model. He is teaching His philosophy of church conduct by a sufficient number of examples to prove that the Holy Spirit's actual, active, present guidance and control is a possible, feasible blessing, because it is in these cases, at least, an indisputable fact. And the Boston pastor to whom reference has been made emphatically said that nothing was more remarkable to him than the fact that, feeling conscious of a lack in himself of what is called "executive ability," he was the more led to humble dependence on the administration of the Spirit; and that from that time forth the Spirit conspicuously led, prompting whom He would to originate various forms of missionary activity at home and abroad; until, without any human planning and without any apparent effort, missions among the Chinese and the Jews, intemperate men and outcast women, and various other neglected classes, sprang up spontaneously and were sustained without anxiety. Then came, as of its own accord, a large training school for Christian workers, where hundreds are yearly taught; and then new missions abroad. Surely it is worthwhile to sacrifice any worldly interests or secular methods if we may thus come to know what meaning there is in that sacred phrase, *"to the Holy Ghost and to us."*

---

73.   Acts 15:28.
74.   Acts 15:25.
75.   Rev. A. J. Gordon, D.D.
76.   Eph. 5:19; Col. 3:16.

10

The Restraint and Constraint of the Spirit

NEW SURPRISES CONSTANTLY meet us in this book. And in this sixteenth chapter we find among the acts of the Holy Ghost both restraint and constraint—prohibition and permission.

This is a new character or function of the Spirit. Paul and Timothy were "forbidden of the Holy Ghost to preach the Word in Asia," and when they "assayed to go into Bithynia;. . .*the Spirit suffered them not.*"[77] The language is explicit. Why thus hindered or diverted does not clearly appear, unless this territory was reserved for other laborers, other methods, other times. For some reason, which it is easy to conjecture were we now dealing with conjectures, God's set and full time had not come. And so, notwithstanding their purpose and endeavor, they were "forbidden," "not suffered." We are twice told that the restraint was of the Holy Spirit.

Side by side with this act of restraint we must, however, place what immediately follows. Paul is

guided by a vision to *go into Macedonia*. The vision
must have been very vivid and unmistakable, for he
adds, "Immediately we endeavored to go into Macedonia, assuredly gathering that the Lord had called
us for to preach the gospel unto them."[78] And so
confident was he of the call that although, instead of
the open doors he had looked for, he and Silas found
the strange welcome of the cruel scourge, the inner
prison, and the torturing stocks, they made the
prison cell echo and ring with midnight songs of
praise, until the Philippian jail became heaven's gate!

Here again we are taught a new and vital lesson.
The Holy Spirit is shown to us in another of His acts
of administration: the double guidance of the
Apostle and his companion; on the one hand *prohibition and restraint*, on the other *permission and constraint*.
They are forbidden in one direction, invited in
another; one way the Spirit says, "Go not"; the other
He calls, "Come"—not into Bithynia, where they
assayed to go, but into Macedonia, where He had a
mission for them to accomplish in introducing the
gospel into Europe.

Many a time in history has supernatural restraint
and constraint changed the course of God's servants. Livingstone assayed to go into China, but
God suffered him not, and sent him to Africa to be
its missionary general, statesman, explorer. Before
him, Carey planned to go to the Great Polynesia in
the South Seas, but God guided him to India to lay

foundations for giving a vernacular Bible to one-sixth of the people of the world. Judson did go to India, but was driven to Burma, where he built up an apostolic church for all the age. Barnabas Shaw was thrust out from Boerland, and trusted to God's guidance of his kine and cart, not knowing whither he went, until the twenty-eighth day brought to him the chief of Namaqualand, his "man of Macedonia," who literally said, "Come over and help us." How many secrets of leading are yet to be brought to light, thousands of God's servants having been forbidden of Him to follow out their plans, because He has had some unexpected open door of service to set before them! And how we need to trust Him for guidance and rejoice equally in His restraints and constraints; because if we had infinite wisdom and love to guide us, we should not by one hair's breadth change His perfect plan for our lives!

In the case of Lydia, "whose heart the Lord opened, that she attended unto the things which were spoken of Paul,"[79] though no direct mention is made of the Spirit, it was one of His acts to open her ears and heart to the gospel. Here again may be read between the lines the Spirit's working, as also in the strongly contrasted case of the jailer at Philippi, and later on in the active search of the Bereans into the Holy Scriptures, so that many of them believed. In Paul's "stirred" spirit at Athens, a mightier Spirit was at work; and in the conversion of that solitary

Areopagite, Dionysius, and that woman, Damaris, who, even in the idolatrous, philosophical, and self-sufficient Attican capital, believed and clave unto Paul, we may see the brooding influence of that same Creator Spirit who over the primal chaos hovered to bring life out of the abyss of death.

We meet in the eighteenth chapter, verse five, a phrase: "Paul was pressed in the spirit"—unless the alternate reading, "engrossed with the Word" (enlogo) is the true one; and we are told that Apollos was "fervent in the spirit,"[80] as also that Paul "purposed in the spirit."[81] These and some other kindred expressions have been thought by some wise Bible students to refer to the Holy Spirit's acting on the mind and heart, creating a holy pressure which must find vent in testimony, a spiritual ardor and fervor which must be relieved by preaching and teaching, or a purpose which was not of the will of man nor of the will of the flesh, but of the will of God. However this be, it is beyond all doubt that in all our inward movings of conviction and affection, of yearning and praying, of determination and decision, we may, in proportion as we maintain close fellowship with Him and are surrendered to Him for service, recognize with joyfulness His acting and actuating.

In this latter purpose of Paul to go to Jerusalem and Rome may be found a possible explanation of his steadfastness of resolve. When at Miletus he was held fast by the Ephesian elders, and in Cesarea,

Agabus prophesied that at the sacred city he should be bound and delivered over to the will of the Gentiles, so that he was tenderly besought not to go up to Jerusalem at all, he "would not be persuaded," and his entreating friends, compelled to desist, could only say, "the will of the Lord be done." Such persistence of purpose seems due not to mere obstinacy, for we are told that Paul went, "bound in the spirit."[82] The same Holy Ghost, who witnessed in every city that bonds and afflictions awaited him, molded his purpose and kept him in the bonds of holy resoluteness and fixedness of heart in doing and suffering the will of God, though, like his Master, he could say, "How am I straitened till it be accomplished!"[83]

The book we are studying shows us that even in disciples there may be entire ignorance, instead of knowledge of the Spirit.

The four marked examples of pentecostal blessing recorded in this book of the acts of the Holy Ghost, of which we now reach the last, have conspicuous differences as well as coincidences.[84] The Spirit never seems exactly to repeat Himself in His operations. Before, we have met His outpourings upon Jews, Samaritans, and Romans; now it is at Ephesus, not Jerusalem, Samaria, or Cesarea, and upon Greeks. The signs are similar, for these Ephesian disciples "spake with tongues, and prophesied."[84] But the *differences* in these four outpourings or effusions are *distinctions*.

At Jerusalem the baptism fell upon apostles and disciples who had received Christian baptism with water and were looking and praying for the Spirit's enduement. In Samaria the Spirit was bestowed on believing converts, newly saved, and who knew of His work at Jerusalem and probably craved similar blessings, though they may not have expected them, being themselves a despised race. In Cesarea the Spirit came upon a whole congregation of Gentile hearers in advance of Christian baptism or confession of Christ, and for the first time *converting and anointing* acts seem to have been simultaneous.

But now, in Ephesus, there is a like manifestation of power, but under new conditions; for there appears to be no exact repetition in spiritual bestowments. These disciples have believed, but have not been instructed, nor "so much as heard whether there be any Holy Ghost."[85] They have never received Christian baptism, but only that of John, which was a baptism *"unto repentance."* They are therefore baptized into Christ, and immediately baptized with the Spirit also.

If we have nothing more, we have both a most instructive lesson on the *possible ignorance of the Holy Spirit's acts*, even on the part of a true disciple of Christ, and an instructive example of the *variety of the Spirit's working*. Think of being a subject of the regenerative act of the Spirit and yet not knowing whether there be any Holy Spirit! The new-born child of God knows not and recognizes not his spiritual Begetter! What a challenge to those who preach and teach the gospel to see that disciples shall not grow up in ignorance of the Spirit's character and work! Yet in how many churches is there systematic teaching upon the third Person of the Trinity?

And again, as to the *variety* of the Spirit's working, what catholic charity and comprehensive hopefulness we are taught! The subjects of Holy Ghost power we may find not only in intelligent disciples, but in outcast Samaritans, in unconverted but inquiring strangers and foreigners, and in un-taught converts who have got to repentance, but not to true knowledge of Christ, and who have never yet known that there is a Holy Spirit. What a boundless encouragement to the missionary to feel that, whether sent to Jew or Gentile, to outcast Pariahs or Athenian philosophers, to unconverted idolaters or nominal Christians bound in the fetters of an igno-rant and servile formalism, the same Spirit of God has blessing everywhere ready to be bestowed; a new Pentecost waiting to be outpoured amid the jungles of India or on the banks of the Congo; on the followers of the false prophet or the disciples of the Chinese sage; on cannibal savages or educated skeptics! We have only to preach the Word and pray in the name of Christ, and the blessed effusion will follow.

And how much depends upon the knowledge and reception of the Spirit we may learn in part from the wonderful "revival" that followed the Pentecost at Ephesus. The signs wrought among believers were succeeded by even more wonderful signs among unbelievers.

In that city and shrine of Diana and of her famous fane, gathered and clustered the magicians, masters of curious and occult arts. Even *they* are turned unto God. And there is a holocaust of the books which contained the very secrets of these "black arts." "Fifty thousand pieces of silver"—an immense fortune for those days—is the estimated value of the books or scrolls burned before all men as a sacrifice for the sake of a new-found Saviour and as a testimony to the power of the gospel. Well might Demetrius and his fellow-craftsmen be alarmed when the "Word of God" so "mightily grew and prevailed,"[86] and feel their trade to be in danger, and even Diana's supremacy to be at risk!

Whenever and wherever disciples get the baptism of power, the enduement from on high, the filling of the Holy Spirit, awakenings and revivals are sure to follow—nay, they have begun. And this chapter teaches us all a permanent lesson: that when disciples have a true *revival*, society gets a *revolution*. When the Spirit moves mightily upon children of God we may look for other mighty movements among unbelievers, and need not be surprised if the devil himself comes down, having great wrath, as though he knew that his time were short.

One more direct reference to the Spirit completes the acts of the Holy Ghost. Paul says to the Ephesian elders, *"Take heed. . .to the flock over the which the Holy Ghost hath made you overseers"*—bishops (episcapoi).[87] And so we come, toward the end of this brief book, to the same lesson emphasized toward its beginning: whatever office one holds in the body of Christ, and whatever men may have to do with selecting and ordaining officers, the Holy Ghost's appointment and authority lie back of all true official service.

We need scarcely tarry on this thought, which we have before expanded, save for the emphasis of *repetition*, which for purposes of conviction has been said to be the "only figure of speech which is worth a farthing." But what calamity can befall a church of Christ greater than this: that its practical administration shall fall into unholy hands—into hands of unspiritual and even unconverted men, who, whatever their worldly qualities or qualifications, lack that one most essential requisite, the power to discern the mind of the Spirit, and so the ability and disposition to cooperate with Him!

Why is this the closing lesson in these acts of the Holy Ghost? Because the one grand purpose of this book is to teach us that the one Head of every true church is the invisible Head; that the church is a body of believers indwelt by the Holy Spirit and administered by Him; that of all important things this is the vital matter—that every officer from pastor to sexton, and every member, shall be a subordinate and servant of this unseen presiding Officer; and that the power to discern this divine Archbishop as in actual control, and setting over His church whomsoever He will, is the fundamental question of fitness for such service. Who that is blinded to spiritual truth can detect the invisible Leader? What if Joshua at Jericho had been unable to see and recognize, or unwilling to obey and follow, that "Captain of the Lord's host" who was present on the field to organize victory!

---

77.   Acts 16:6-7.
78.   Acts 16:10.
79.   Acts 16:14.
80.   Acts 18:25.
81.   Acts 19:21.
82.   Acts 20:22.
83.   Luke 12:50.
84.   Acts 19:6.
85.   Acts 19:2.
86.   Acts 19:20.
87.   Acts 20:28.

11

Conclusion—The Reception and Rejection of the Spirit

NO BLESSING, THOUGH IT be the richest God can give and the most needful man can have, is forced upon our acceptance. It is a fact fraught with solemn significance that the book which thus opens with the Holy Spirit, and is pervaded throughout with His presence and power, also closes with Him, only the promise of the first chapter turns into a warning in the last. Notwithstanding the marvels wrought in this first generation of church history, there were some who called themselves God's people and prided themselves on their "election," who were blind, deaf, hardhearted, and lost their golden opportunity. Even when such a man as Paul the aged, expounded and testified the kingdom of God, persuading them concerning Jesus, both out of the law of Moses and out of the prophets, from morning till evening, it is sadly recorded that while "some believed the things which were spoken,. . .some believed not."[88] And, as they departed, not to give simple faith its blessed exercise in believing and trusting, but to indulge their wayward minds and have great reasonings among themselves, the Apostle gave utterance once more to that awful rebuke of the prophet Isaiah,[89] which is more forcible, and probably more intelligible, if translated so as to bring out the *voluntary* element in this willful rejection of testimony:

"Go unto this people, and say,
Hearing ye will hear, and will not understand;
And seeing ye will see, and will not perceive:
For the heart of this people is waxed gross,
And their ears are dull of hearing,
And their eyes have they closed;
Lest they should see with their eyes,
And hear with their ears,
And understand with their heart,
And should turn about,
And I should heal them."

These words were addressed by Paul, not to ordinary unregenerate sinners, but to selected and representative Jewish hearers, to the professed people of God, to backslidden believers; and in that fact is a doubly emphatic word of warning, which, like a sledgehammer striking upon God's anvil of judgment, admonishes us that for similar sins of rejection God may enter into controversy with His people in these times also.

Is it possible that, even in our own day, with the burning chapters of the acts of the Holy Ghost open before our eyes, compelling us to read their perpetual lesson, we may yet come under the same condemnation? Is it possible that the heart of believers is waxed gross, and their ears are dull of hearing, and their eyes they have closed; so that while they cannot but see this marvelous testimony, they have no real spiritual perception, understanding, or disposition to accept the teaching of this book? Can it be that the church of Christ has practically denied to the Spirit of God His rightful seat of authority and administration, and put in His place a usurper—the spirit of this world which worketh in the children of disobedience? It is a solemn question, which—without daring, or even desiring, to bring against any of God's professed people a railing accusation—we can only ask every believer, minister of Christ, and church to consider; for it is to this inquiry that all our studies of this Book of the Acts must finally lead.

Certain it is that the power of the Holy Spirit no longer pervades our witness and work as of old. We have risen from these studies of the acts of the Holy Spirit with an unquenchable desire to see this power once more manifested. We are not zealous or jealous for the particular *form* and mode in which the Spirit's presence shall be exhibited, nor that the exact signs and wonders of the apostolic age should be revived. God has infinite variety of manifestations, and the particular modes of that manifestation may vary as the times and needs change. But the Holy Spirit was given that He may abide with the church forever; and we cannot believe that so glorious and divine a person as the Spirit of God dwells in the church and yet gives no unmistakable sign or signal of His presence. There has been promised one "everlasting sign that shall not be cut off."[90] The thorn shall still be displaced by the fir tree, and the brier by the myrtle tree; plants of godliness shall spring up in unpromising soils and bear celestial fruit, that He may be glorified.[91]

If the Spirit dwells in the body of Christ, and is left free to work His own will, He will quicken the whole body. Members will have a new care one for another, suffering and rejoicing together. There will be a holy jealousy for the welfare and happiness of all who belong to the mystical body, and an earnest and loving cooperation in all holy work. All schism, whether manifest in inward estrangement or in outward separation, becomes impossible where the Spirit of Love prevails; all heresy becomes impossible so far as the Spirit of Truth indwells; and all apathy and inactivity in the face of a dying world will give way to sympathetic activity when and so far as the Spirit of Life thrills the body; even as all ignorance of God and superstitious worship of forms flee like owls of the night when the Spirit of Light shines in His divine splendor. In a word, all needs of the church are met so surely and speedily as the Holy Ghost, who still abides in the church as God's only earthly temple, resumes by the consent and cooperation of disciples His normal control, actively guiding into all truth and duty.

The question we are raising is immensely practical. Upon its answer everything hangs which concerns the power of the church for God. Let us suppose that a wave of divine revival should sweep over the land, and that a prayerful spirit of candid self-search, should be its result; that pastors, church officers, church members, should unite to purge the courts of God of all idols of the world; that the service of song in the house of the Lord should be put into consecrated hands, with a holy jealousy for spiritual praise rather than artistic and esthetic music; that preaching should become a simple declaration of God's testimony in Holy Ghost power; that secular men, however wealthy, cultured, influential, should be displaced in all church offices by disciples who, being filled with the Holy Spirit, could discern His mind and obey His leading; that all worldly methods of raising money for the Lord's work should be abandoned, and voluntary, self-denying offerings, consecrated by prayer, should take their place; that the lost art of prayer in the closet, and in the assemblies of saints, should be restored to its true place, and nothing should be done or attempted without waiting on God until His mind were made known in a word, let us suppose that our whole church life were resolutely remodeled after the pattern showed us in the holy mount; dare any of us to doubt that God would work signs and wonders of grace not less convincing in their way than those wrought in the days of which Pentecost was the glorious dawn?

God's name is "I AM"—mystic name indeed;[92] yet whatever else it means, it can mean no less than this: *one everlasting, unchanging* NOW. He is "the same yesterday, and today, and forever."[93] What He was, He is; what He has done, He can do, will do, *does*, whether or not His being and doing are seen or known by us. Like the sun, His shining is perpetual. We may get into the dark, but the light is essentially undimmed. We may shut out the light, but it is struggling to reach us behind the shutters. The church of God may pass into eclipse behind the world's shadow, but the sun is still as radiant and glorious. There is in God "no variableness, neither shadow of turning." His past deeds, however wonderful, are the promise, prophecy, and proof of what He wills to do and waits to do when our conditions make it possible. And to charge, directly or indirectly, our failures or declensions upon Him, is to charge Him with being a liar, a false promiser, a capricious, changeable, untrustworthy God. Our doubts are denials, and our unbelief is indirect blasphemy, if not apostasy.

In the previous pages we have followed step by step the disclosures of the Holy Spirit's presence and power, with reference to tracing a progressive development of doctrine. It may be well, before we close this brief study, to give a backward glance, and look at the lessons we have learned, not with reference to their chronological order, but to their logical connection; not analytically, but synthetically, that we may see what a comprehensive body of truth we have been taught in these Acts of the Holy Ghost.

These inspired pages contain a very remarkable revelation of the Holy Spirit of God, which may be briefly summarized in twelve particulars:

1. His character as the promised Paraclete, the ascension gift of the Father to the Son, and of the Son to the church which He purchased with His own blood.

2. His descent from heaven, and advent among believers, in four representative outpourings: at Jerusalem in Judea, in Samaria, in Cesarea among Romans, and at Ephesus among Greeks.

3. His power working in His witnesses, in unction and utterance, for preaching and prophesying, in many tongues and tongues of fire; in fullness of grace and boldness of testimony in the face of resolute foes.

4.   His personality and individuality, divinity and diety, so that He is the one and only true Vicar of Christ, of whom it can rightfully be said that He, "as God, sitteth in the temple of God, showing himself that He is God."[94]

5.   His divine agency and activity in bringing to birth the church, the body of Christ, adding believers to the Lord, multiplying them greatly, and making a great company of priests obedient to the faith.

6.   His presence and presidency in the church, making elders His overseers, deacons His distributers of bounty, and all truly obedient souls His subordinates and servants; and deigning to act as a fellow-counselor in a church council, sealing its deliverances with His sanction.

7.   His co-witness with Christ to believers, and with believers to the world; testifying to disciples, in them and through them, glorifying Christ by taking of Christ's and showing to them, and then attesting and approving their word of witness by mighty works and wonders.

8.   His individual leading and dealing, His love for inquiring souls and His guidance of His appointed teachers, bringing one inquirer and one teacher into saving contact; designating by name His chosen messengers to the Gentiles, separating them and sending them forth, then restraining and constraining them as to their fields of labor.

9. His power over hearers, so that they were pricked or cut to the heart by the sword of the Spirit; demonstrating the truth; convincing of sin, of righteousness, of judgment; making men to tremble; leading them to repent, believe, and be baptized; to confess their deeds, renounce their curious arts, and burn their costly books before all men.

10. His holy jealousy for honesty, and for His own honor, punishing those who lied to the Holy Ghost and agreed to tempt Him by defrauding Him of devoted things; avenging such insults to His divine person by instant judgments, so that great fear came not only upon the church, but upon as many as heard these things.

11. His *paraclesis* or complete administration in the body of Christ, so that the Word of God increased, the church had rest, was both multiplied and edified, and saints continued steadfastly in the apostles' doctrine and fellowship, in breaking of bread, and in prayers, and were of one heart and of one soul.

12. His impartations and revelations to disciples, increasing their faith and joy in the Holy Ghost, teaching them what they should speak, and anointing them for faithful utterance; making them strong to serve and suffer, and so filling them that they could not but speak, and rejoiced to suffer shame for His name.

In addition to all this we have found here a

promise of another time of refreshing, dependent, not on the absence, but the presence of the Lord; a latter rain when the Spirit shall be poured out on all flesh, and all things shall be fulfilled which were spoken by all His holy prophets since the world began.

Church of Christ! the records of these acts of the Holy Ghost have never reached completeness. This is the one book which has no proper close, because it waits for new chapters to be added so fast and so far as the people of God shall reinstate the blessed Spirit in His holy seat of control. He will occupy no disputed throne and exercise no divided sovereignty. He will tolerate no "idols of the tribe, the den, the marketplace, the theater,"[95] in His courts. A worldly and unspiritual church is a church that practically has not the Spirit; and not to have the Spirit is to languish, to have a name to live while dead, to lose light and life, truth and love, peace and power:

"Gideon's fleece" suggests a double lesson: there may be blessed moisture from heavenly dews while all is dry about us, and there may be accursed dryness while all is moisture about us. While we pray for the whole body of Christ, our responsibility is individual. Let us cultivate divine fellowship in the Spirit, yield ourselves unto God as those who are alive from the dead, and dare to take a bold but loving stand for Holy Ghost administration in the church, that He may be welcomed to His rightful seat of sovereignty; and beneath His golden scepter every blessing shall distil like the dew, and the Lord shall anew command His blessing, even life forevermore!

---

88.   Acts 28:23-24.
89.   Isa. 6:9-10.
90.   Isa. 55:13.
91.   Isa. 60:21; 61:11.
92.   Exod. 3:14.
93.   Heb. 13:8.
94.   2 Thess. 2:4.
95.   Francis Bacon.